LOVING PRAYER

A Study Guide to Everyday Jewish Prayer

LOVING PRAYER

A Study Guide to Everyday Jewish Prayer

Tamar Frankiel

Gaon Books
www.gaonbooks.com
Loving Prayer: A Study Guide to Everyday Jewish Prayer.
Tamar Frankiel. Copyright (c) 2017. All rights reserved. This
publication is in copyright.

For permissions, group pricing, and other information con-
tact Gaon Books, P.O. Box 23924, Santa Fe, NM 87502 or write
(gaonbooks@gmail.com). Gaon Books is an imprint of Gaon Institute for Tolerance Studies, a 501-c-3 non-profit organization.

Manufactured in the United States of America.

The paper used in this publication is acid free and meets
all ANSI (American National Standards for Information Sci-
ences) standards for archival quality paper. All wood product
components used in this book are Sustainable Forest Initiative
(SFI) certified.

Library of Congress Cataloging-in-Publication Data

Names: Frankiel, Tamar, 1946- author.
Title: Loving prayer : a study guide to everyday Jewish prayer
/ Tamar Frankiel.
Description: Santa Fe, New Mexico : Gaon Books, [2016]
Identifiers: LCCN 2016037614 | ISBN 9781935604815 (pbk. :
alk. paper)
Subjects: LCSH: Prayer--Judaism. | Shaharit.
Classification: LCC BM669 .F645 2016 | DDC 296.4/5--dc23
LC record available at https://lccn.loc.gov/2016037614

Table Of Contents

Preface

This book is for you if you want to enhance your understanding and practice of our Jewish prayer tradition. It is a study guide, offering new perspectives to refresh your approach and give guidance in complexity of prayer and its meanings. Prayer is, after all, a key part of our ancient spiritual practice, but it can be difficult for modern Jews to find their way into it. The siddur or prayer book may seem too dense. You may lose interest easily and need a framework that sustains your involvement. You might be already familiar with the prayers, but they have become rote for you – you need some new insights.

I've had some of the same experiences. I began learning the prayers with an excitement about learning something new, including learning to read Hebrew at the same time. I struggled to follow the service while enjoying its songs and rhythms. Over time I became more comfortable, and began to experience a period of deep engagement with the prayers. I prayed on my own much of the time. When we had the opportunity to pray with a community, on a holiday or special Shabbat, it was glorious.

But that was followed by years of much less attention to prayers, for I was now a working mother with five children. We lived in an active Jewish community but I had so little time, and often just rushed through a few formal prayers. I became interested in Jewish meditation, which helped for a while. Still, over the years my own practice waxed and waned: sometimes I was actively davening every morning, while at other times I was speaking to God less, studying and contemplating more.

My opportunities to teach enriched my own prayers, but I was well aware that for many, many Jews, the prayer book was still opaque. They felt stymied by the language, the length of the prayers, and their own theological questions. I wanted to share my love for the prayers, but I was not sure how to move beyond the existing books and viewpoints. After years of teaching, the weekday morning prayers opened up to me at another level. This book is the result. I'm grateful to my students in *tefillah* at the Academy for Jewish Religion, California, without whom I might not have persisted in finding new ways of understanding our prayers.

We begin with the consciousness that Jewish prayer is a liturgy, best thought of as a cousin to drama, dance, or symphony. It is not someone's spontaneous prayer written down for others to imitate. Liturgy is composed, crafted, arranged for a purpose. I like the analogy of drama because I can think of the segments of liturgy as scenes. The comparison also invites me to identify with characters or actions as well as to contemplate ideas and themes.

As a practitioner, you are a performer in the drama. Just as you might learn a part for a Shakespeare play, you will appreciate the liturgical drama more when you have prepared, when you know the whole play from start to finish even though your part seems small. Though some performances will seem just ordinary, there will be moments when you are swept up in the grand movement of it all. Best of all, there's no audition required; you can join the cast at any time; and it's the longest running play in the world.

A certain kind of consciousness will develop as you take on this approach to practice: an imaginative interaction with the words of the siddur. Unlike a play that you watch from the audience, much of the liturgical drama goes on in your imagination. Actually, we are using our imaginations with a stage play as well – we "identify" with the characters and our bodies respond with pleasure or sadness or thrill to the action, in empathic imagination. With Jewish prayer, we need to extract the drama from the words before us and carry it along in our minds, as well as attend to our feelings and inner senses.

While that may seem odd at first, think of High Holy Day prayers. There, the drama is fleshed out more fully in the *machzor* (holiday prayer book), with the conceptual framework of crowning a king on Rosh Hashanah, and the readings about ancient atonement sacrifices on Yom Kippur. A musical score accompanies the congregation, and the cantor sings with great emotion. We are absolutely expected to identify imaginatively with the prospect of being recorded in the Book of Life, and with the sheep that pass before the shepherd in the *Unetaneh tokef* prayer:

> *As a shepherd herds his flock, causing his sheep to pass beneath his staff, so do You cause to pass, count, and record, visiting the souls of all living, decreeing the length of their days, . . .*

Indeed, many rabbis and teachers insist that *koach ha-dimyon*, the power of the imagination, is essential to a dynamic spirituality. Guided meditations or visualizations have been used in prayer and in private Jewish spiritual practice for centuries. The words of our prayers often invite the imaginative effort – we almost involuntarily try to imagine unity when we concentrate on the *Shema* and pronounce the word *"echad."* In the spiritual approach proposed in this book, we are applying imagination more consciously, engaging more fully with what is before us in the text.

Using this book fully, then, will require not just reading it beginning to end, but sitting down with the siddur at the same time. I will point to a prayer but not necessarily quote it in its entirety. Rather, I will be calling your attention to things you may not otherwise notice – a word, a phrase, a poetic structure, the interweaving of a whole section of prayers. So it's best if you have a copy of a traditional siddur at hand and be ready to open it as you read. (I will remind you from time to time.)

When I say "traditional" siddur, I mean an orthodox or conservative siddur that has a full version of the prayers. I will give page numbers for the Koren-Sacks siddur (Ashkenaz) – a very recent version of a traditional prayer book translated by Rabbi Jonathan Sacks, former chief rabbi of England, who has a superb command of contemporary English idiom. You can use another siddur; you just will not have the same page numbers. Reform and Reconstructionist siddurim may not give a complete version of the weekday prayer service, or may use a translation that varies so much that it would confuse you as the reader of this book. Nevertheless, you will eventually be able to adapt what you learn to those and many other formats and presentations.

Transmitted in Hebrew, the liturgy carries its own inherent barrier that is sometimes formidable to cross. Fortunately, translations into other languages are available and, in English, they are increasingly accessible and helpful. You do not need to know Hebrew to use this book; when I refer to Hebrew words or phrases, they are transliterated in a manner common to popular Jewish literature rather than scholarly customs. The English translations of the prayers in this book may differ somewhat from the Koren version, as I have sometimes used other sources to capture a certain flavor in the Hebrew. A simple example is that the phrase "You are great" is the most familiar English idiom, but I might choose the Hebrew word order and translate "Great are You." In some cases a particular choice of a word is intended to bring out the root meaning of a Hebrew word that might not otherwise be obvious. I encourage my students to compare many translations of prayers and I hope you will do the same.

Another issue that arises for Jewish prayers in English is how to translate the Tetragrammaton or four-letter Name of God. Since the King James Version of the (Christian) Bible, a practice has prevailed of substituting the word "Lord." This actually reflects Jewish practice of substituting "*Adonai*," which literally translates as "my Lord." However, Jews tend not to use "Lord" in actual prayer because to us it sounds Christian. Still, "*Adonai*" has had, for centuries, the status of a holy name, such that we don't want to use it too casually. What to do?

I have chosen to write *Adonai* as the substitute for the four-letter Name when it occurs in prayers, because that is what we would say if we were praying. Most teachers accept that we may say it in practicing reading or studying the siddur as a holy text. In discussing a prayer, you may want to use another term such as *Hashem* (literally, "the name") in order to preserve the unique status of the name *Adonai*.

When providing biblical citations, or quoting from another source besides the actual prayers, I have preserved the custom of translating the four-letter Name as "Lord," since that is how you will usually see it if you go to an English Tanakh or secondary source. With the name *Elohim* and its variants, (*Elohai, Elohenu*), even though it is also a holy name, it has long been accepted to translate it simply as "God," both in prayers and elsewhere.

Prayer is a Jewish spiritual practice – but one may well ask, what is it practice for? There is an answer: it is practice for living a life imbued with depth, awareness, sensitivity, ethical consciousness and compassion – a combination we appropriately label "spirituality." Growing in depth and breadth of consciousness requires gaining understanding and knowledge. To increase sensitivity, our practice must continually promote humility and openness to the mystery of being. To engage compassion and ethical consciousness, it must increase awareness of the larger wholes of which we are a part. And, as a specifically Jewish spiritual practice, the prayers we say must be grounded in awareness of the inter-relationships of our individual selves, our community, God, Torah, and the Jewish people.

Like any form of practice (think of a musical instrument or physical exercise), spiritual practice works best when it is frequent; thus most forms of spiritual practice have a daily component as well as seasons of the year when practice is intensified. It also works best when disciplined in content, yet variable enough – including variations introduced by the practitioner – to avoid boredom. Jewish prayer has all these qualities.

The positive effects of this spiritual practice are innumerable. I invite you to trust, experiment, and enjoy.

Mah Tovu

How good are your tents, Yaakov! And your dwelling
places, Israel!
And I --
through Your abundant kindness
I will enter Your house
I will bow toward Your holy sanctuary
in awe of You.
Adonai,
I love the house where You reside,
the dwelling place of Your glory.
And I --
I will bow, and kneel, and bend before *Adonai*
my Maker.
And I –
my prayer is to You, *Adonai*
at a time of desire --
God, in Your abundant kindness
answer me
in the truth of Your salvation.[1]

Chapter 1

Introduction

The Unique Components of Our Prayer

Dramatic compositions have structure – Shakespeare habitually wrote plays in five acts. Characters spoke in soliloquies and choruses as well as dialogue. He used a signature poetic metric, iambic pentameter, punctuating it occasionally with prose.

In a parallel way, Jewish liturgy has characteristic components. Here they are:

- The weekday morning service, which is our template, has four main sections, usually titled in English: Morning Blessings; Verses of Song; the *Shema* and Its Blessings; the Eighteen Blessings (or, Standing Prayer).
- Different genres may be used within a section, ranging from single verses from the Tanakh (Bible), to long quotations, to poetic compositions. Music has been composed over many centuries, also in different styles and tempos. This ensures diversity, but it can be difficult at first because you don't know what to expect next.
- The rabbis who assembled and composed the prayer book were immersed in Tanakh (Bible), so knowing something of the biblical background helps to decode the prayers and their interrelationships. Most contemporary English translations offer biblical references for the reader; but it takes time to search them out. This book provides more access to the biblical background than most treatments of Jewish prayer.

- The signature of Jewish prayer is the blessing or *brachah* (alternately transliterated as *berakhah* or other variants), known by its formulaic beginning, *Baruch ata Adonai*.... or "Blessed are you, *Adonai* ...." which functions to uphold the structure as well as to convey meaning. When you see a *brachah*, it's often a flag to attend to its place or function as well as its content.

- Our prayers have a largely unnoticed circular structure which relates various parts to one another and creates an internal, unconscious experience for the practitioner. Only a few writers on the siddur have mentioned this structure (technically called by the literary term chiasmus), but I will spend time explaining it and call attention to it frequently. Making this structure more conscious enhances our awareness of the meaning of the prayers.

- Just as a play may have a main story and subplots, or a symphony has a theme and variations, Jewish prayers have themes that recur throughout, such as creation, love, revelation, redemption from evil.

- The main story, however, is implicit rather than explicit: it is a mystical journey and thus, in traditional language, a "secret." In the four sections of morning prayer, the practitioner is guided through a spiritual story, one that involves traversing four "worlds" of meaning. Those worlds can provide a grounding and centering for one's day as well as a point of reference for spiritual growth. These four worlds were identified by Jewish mystics some two thousand years ago, and have served as a spiritual framework for serious seekers ever since. We will begin there.

Drama of the Four Worlds

Whereas secular drama evolved toward telling stories around social and political relations or individual struggles, liturgies developed a vocabulary for the transcendent. Relations between God or the gods and humans may have begun with the drama of sacrifices conceived of as gifts or transactions, but over the centuries rituals came to express the intimate relationship of a community and its individual members to God.

The vocabulary of Four Worlds, which the Jewish tradition offers to explore our relationship to God, came from the ancient tradition of mysticism known as *Ma'aseh Merkavah*, the "work of the chariot." *Merkavah* or "chariot" refers to the vision of the biblical prophet Yechezkel, known in English as Ezekiel, and it is the opening chapter of his book. We read this chapter in synagogue on the holiday of Shavuot, as the Haftarah (prophetic reading) for the day, because our sages saw it as parallel to or reminiscent of the giving of the Torah itself.

Ezekiel, a priest (*kohen*) who had been exiled to Babylonia along with thousands of other Jews after the destruction of the First Temple in 586 B.C.E., reports that he was standing by the river Chebar and saw a vision of a chariot descending from the sky. The chariot's components were not mechanical, but rather various kinds of living beings, usually understood as angels -- but not of the type familiar from Renaissance paintings. The wheels or *ofanim* were alive, the corner posts called *chayot* were alive, and there was a "likeness of a man" in the center where the rider would be. The appearance of the various parts of the chariot unfolded as though it were being revealed level by level, emerging from the clouds, and the top of the anthropomorphic figure, whom Ezekiel referred to as God, could not be seen. The vision was accompanied by sounds and light and color. It was oriented toward the four directions, and the beings may be correlated with astrological symbols.

At a time when the people had just lost their Temple, which in ancient times was the fundamental means of connecting to God, this was an enormous message of hope. God was riding on the cosmic chariot toward them! The chariot vision recreated their link to God, bringing a substitute for the Temple to the people in exile.

The mystics in meditating and reflecting on this text developed the concept of various worlds linking the earthly with the heavenly. This idea was already known in Talmudic times (2nd-6th centuries C.E.) and was elaborated and clarified down through the Middle Ages by those who came to be known as "kabbalists." (*Kabbalah* means the "received" tradition.)

The four parts of the prayer service are actually our gateway to this mystical path, through the Four Worlds derived from Ezekiel's vision. These four dimensions of prayer offer us the opportunity to make a *tikkun* (correction) for our individual and collective lives, which all too often are distortions of the divine intention.

What are these worlds? We'll start with a chart which can help you visualize them. Think of them as the scenery or staging of a play, providing an environment in which certain things can and typically do happen. In a play, a scene taking place inside a room offers certain kinds of interactions, while an outdoor scene is likely to suggest something else. A playwright might create a storm as in King Lear, or a laboratory for Dr. Jekyll. Each of the four worlds is likewise a world, but not merely an imaginary one.

The Hebrew vocabulary of the Four Worlds is helpful. Starting from the top, the worlds are:

- *Atzilut*, from the root *a.tz.l* meaning "near" or noble, designates a realm of closeness to the divine that we do not ordinarily experience.
- *Beriah*, from the root *b.r.a*, means creation. It is the word used in the first verse of the Torah, "At the beginning, God created the heavens and the earth."
- *Yetzirah*, from the root *y.tz.r*, means shaping or formation.
- *Asiyah*, from the verb *a.s.h*, means doing or action. This is the "lowest" world, and most familiar to us in everyday life.

The diagram on the next page represents the Four Worlds in a capsule format.

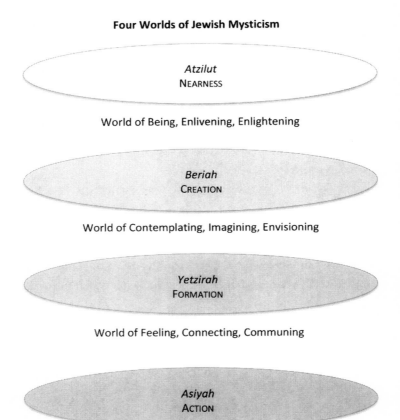

Four Worlds of Jewish Mysticism

Atzilut
NEARNESS

World of Being, Enlivening, Enlightening

Beriah
CREATION

World of Contemplating, Imagining, Envisioning

Yetzirah
FORMATION

World of Feeling, Connecting, Communing

Asiyah
ACTION

World of Doing, Producing, Measuring, Acting

Starting from the lowest world, with which we are most familiar, we can briefly describe these spiritual stage-scenes.

ASIYAH. The lowest world is called the world of *Asiyah*, Doing or Action. Probably 75 percent of our consciousness is occupied with this world of doingness: What will we do today? What is our role? How do things work? How can we accomplish our desires and finish what we have planned? Goal-orientation is a significant part of *asiyah*-consciousness; and our interactions with others are usually to get them to work with us on goals, or to compete with them in accomplishing goals. If you imagine a complicated and demanding work environment – an aerodynamics corporation with a factory, corporate offices, customers, engineers, you get the basic idea of *Asiyah*.

All the "things that we do" carry with them attitudes and beliefs. A primary belief in this world is the principle of cause and effect: the cause comes before the effect in linear time, and the cause "makes" the effect happen. (*Asiyah* can also mean 'making.') We take this so much for granted that we hardly realize it is simply a belief, true in this situation but not necessarily in all realities. We can imagine, for example, a world with time-travel, for example, that would deny cause and effect as being one-directional.

This world is alluded to by the angels called *ofanim* or "wheels" of the chariot vision. Comparatively, we might think of the Hindu-Buddhist concept of the world of *samsara*, the wheel of death and rebirth which eternally goes on, each action causing another.[2] Some traditions propose a means of escape from this unending wheel of suffering. The Jewish idea, however, is not to escape from the World of Action in some ultimate liberation, but to correct it and harmonize our ordinary action with higher levels of consciousness.

In our spiritual practice, *Asiyah* corresponds to the first section of prayers known as Morning Blessings, *Bircat HaShachar,* where we become aware of all the gifts that make it possible to act in the world, acknowledge them, and give thanks to God for them; thus we prepare ourselves for service. Our expressions of appreciation are a *tikkun* or correction for the World of Action, because gratitude tempers our inclination to think that we are in control or that our goals are the most important realities. Realizing that we are dependent on others, beings and forces that we did not create, shifts our perspective on all our actions, and we can be less ego-invested in the outcomes.

The highlights of the section are a compendium of blessings said daily, although there are a number of other songs and recitations which may be added in one's private practice. In the Koren Siddur (Ashkenaz), the blessings are on pages 4-19 and 26-35. This first scene of the drama is fairly short in our regular services – perhaps because it takes up so much time in the rest of our life! However, blessings are part of Jewish practice on many other occasions, reminding us that gratitude can be our continual grounding. In Chapter 1, we will talk about varieties of blessings.

YETZIRAH. The second world, or Scene II of our drama, is the world of *Yetzirah* or formation. *Yotzer* is a Hebrew word meaning to create, specifically with the idea of shaping something from a malleable substance. If you are familiar with traditional Jewish moral terminology, you might recognize the common linguistic root in *yetzer ha-ra* and *yetzer ha-tov*, the "evil inclination" and the "good inclination." *Yetzer* as inclination in that context implies the way one tends to lean, the shape of one's path toward good or evil.

The world of *Yetzirah* points to tendencies or felt direction, a shape that isn't firmly defined in space-time as physical objects are. It also comprises what we might call the emotional world, broadly speaking – not only each individual response of positive or negative feeling, but also the currents that give shape to our reality, behind the scenes of our visible, tangible, audible actions. In individuals, the *Yetzirah* reality is more like what we call temperament, including our dominating passions and lasting motivations, and also our typical range of sensitivities to various influences.

The world of *Yetzirah* in the collective sense is the locus of emotional exchanges between beings –mostly with other humans, but sometimes with animals or other entities. Although we sometimes explain these in cause-and-effect language ("that made me angry"), emotions often seem to arise and affect others without conscious "making." A comedian intends to make us laugh; but a chill can come over a room, or sadness can be contagious without any intent or goal on anyone's part. When we have telepathic ("feeling-at-a-distance") experiences, these seem not to obey the limitations of space and time, as if they were riding on their own system of connection. In *yetzirah*-consciousness, a different environment seems to be at play, where receptivity and connectedness are more important than decision and accomplishment.

The corresponding part of the prayer service is *Pesukei d'Zimrah*, Verses of Song – a series of biblical verses and psalms that evoke joy, pleasure, enthusiasm, and connection to a wider world full of life. They are supposed to be sung or chanted poetically. Music is the artistic form that most directly engages our emotions, partly because it does not need to be fully translated into words and concepts. Music can make connections between people easier, and so contributes to our receptivity to others. In ancient times, music and poetry were understood to transform consciousness and even to aid in prophecy. Thus the *Pesukei d'Zimrah*, especially with appropriate music, can increase our emotional receptivity. "Music hath charms," and can change the *yetzer*, the inclination of one's passions.

BERIAH. The third world, Scene III, is *Beriah* or creation. This is the realm of thought, word, and image where ideas relate to each other in new and creative ways. It is the doorway to domains where the patterns and archetypes of life emerge, as in dreams. New relationships among ideas, scientific or theoretical creativity, and the various forms of artistic expression spring from a relationship with Beriah. The experiences accompanying creative insights and accomplishments often are described as coming "through" the artist or thinker, or as gifts from some source beyond the person. The nature of *beriah* is such that we do not control it, but rather become aware of a transcendent dimension in creativity.

While we do not control such experiences, we can increase our receptivity to them. Being able to free oneself from preoccupation with ordinary events of life is a start in that direction. Practices of meditation, prayer, contemplation, or deep study (as in Torah study) can decrease the ego-concerns that stand in our way, and thus help a person develop receptivity.

In the prayers, we will see that cosmic creativity and divine love are the themes of the two *brachot* before the *Shema*, setting the stage for the opening of *beriah*-consciousness. As actors in this third scene, we participate by imagining greater realities than our everyday world, expanding our limited view of what is possible. We become connected to the cosmos in its loving nature, and in this process a *tikkun* occurs in our relationship to God. We become aware that the divine-human relationship cannot be based on mere deeds; and our response to divine love and creativity arises from the transformation of our will, rather than from guilt or duty. As we will see, this makes possible a new experience of covenant, as well as a deeper understanding of what is called "redemption."

ATZILUT. The fourth world is known as *Atzilut*, often translated as "emanation," as it referred to the primal source from which everything emanated. However, the root *etzel* in Hebrew means "near" or "noble," as the noble is near to the king. This world offers the ineffable reality of nearness to God, and at the same time it has the potential to be the place where we see ourselves, the world and its needs most clearly. This will be better understood when we study the *Amidah* or Standing Prayer, known as *Shemoneh esreh* ("18") on weekdays. The practice of silent inner listening combines with speaking the words of the great biblical prophets to create this unique prayer, which was called by our sages the Tefillah, the communal prayer for redemption in the world.

The "Ladder of Prayer" below shows you the relationship of the segments of prayer to these worlds.

Four Levels of Morning Prayer

Amidah (Shemoneh esreh)
ATZILUT - SILENT SPEECH

Inspiration, Yearning

Shema and Its Blessings
BERIAH - CREATION AND REDEMPTION

Contemplating Light, Love, Unity, Truth

Pesukei d'Zimrah
YETZIRAH - JOY AND INTERCONNECTEDNESS

Experiencing, Feeling, Singing

Birchot HaShachar, Morning Blessings
ASIYAH - GRATITUDE

Awakening, Appreciating, Awareness

If you are a beginner with Jewish prayer, spend some time every day with focus on one small part. The next day, pick a different prayer or section to focus. You don't have to choose things in order. Think of yourself as an actor in the drama, learning the parts.

Before you start a section, spend a little time recalling what world you are in. When you've read more of this book and become familiar with some of the prayers, you can ask yourself, what's the scene? What's the atmosphere? Who is highlighted? What is your role? You may want to journal about your experience as actor in each scene.

Chapter 2

Blessings:
The Signature of Jewish Prayer

When the Torah recorded that God blessed Adam and Chava (Eve), a bell must have gone off in the garden of souls. "Blessing! That's the key!"

Later, when Abraham was told, "You shall be a blessing," our mission was clear. Still further on in history, our liturgy would mirror this radiant light. The ability to bless and receive blessings would be a cherished aspect of Jewish life, in family, community, and in relation to the divine. The word *berakhah/ brachah* and all its forms would inspire our prayers.

Types of Blessings

(If you are already familiar with the range and format of blessings in Judaism, you may wish to skip this and the next section, and go to "The Architecture of Prayer" on page 35.)

Blessings begin in the Tanakh with God's blessings on fish and on humans, that they should "be fruitful and multiply." This gives us a clue to the Divine definition of blessing: it suggests increase, growth, and fulfillment of potential.

Blessings often have the character of what is called in linguistics a "performative utterance," a phrase or statement that brings about a change. An example is when a judge in a civil marriage says "I now pronounce you husband and wife." By the performative act of saying those words, he has made them different people socially, legally, economically. Statements of this type from God constitute a creative act: "Let there be light" was an utterance that performed an act: "and there was light." In a parallel way, a blessing intends to generate goodness, growth, fulfillment in another being through words that are spoken. A blessing from a human is not a creation in the same sense; but it can draw out previously unexpressed potential in the person or thing blessed.

As we go through the stories of our biblical ancestors, we find many examples of God blessing them, or they blessing others; for example:

> *The Lord said to Avram, ..."I will make of you a great nation, and I will bless you"... (Genesis 12:1, 2).*
> *And Isaac called Jacob and blessed him, ...and said..."May God Almighty bless you and make you fruitful and multiply..." (Genesis 28: 1, 3).*
> *And Melchizedek king of Salem . . .blessed him and said, "Blessed be Avram by God Most High" (Genesis 14: 18, 19).*

The last example is illustrative. Avraham (then called Avram; Abraham in English) had already shown his ability to fight like a warrior, and indeed appeared blessed by God. Melchizedek, an ancient priest of Salem, was in effect amplifying the demonstrated blessing by his statement. According to tradition, the priestly blessing given to Aaron to say was the continuation of this tradition. The *kohanim* renew God's blessing on Israel each time they say the Priestly Blessing, evoking the unique potential of each person and the people as a whole.[3]

Occasionally in the Tanakh, we find people blessing God: Melchizedek also said, "Blessed be God!" Or in the book of Ruth, "And Naomi said to Ruth, 'Blessed be God.'" This is a different use of the word blessing. The humans in these cases are not blessing the Divine, in the sense that the Divine would become literally "greater." Most interpreters read it as an expression of thanksgiving, which certainly is appropriate.

One can also read it as praise: Blessed/praised be God, and may God's "name" be greater among human beings (because of what God has done here). This fits with the biblical emphasis on "making God's name great" among the nations. We see this in the story of Abraham, who set up altars and "called on the name of the Lord" (Genesis 12.8). Classically, in the stories in Exodus of the redemption from Egypt, concern for God's "name" is at the forefront: "That the nations will not say, 'He could not bring them out so He killed them in the wilderness.'" To "bless God" is to exalt God in one's own eyes and others, that is, to increase awareness of God in the universe.

Thus when God blesses a person, or a parent blesses a child, or the *kohanim* bless the congregation in a prayer service, they are performing an act intended to bring out the hidden potential in the person. When we bless God, we are simultaneously expressing thanks and intending to make the Divine presence, and particularly God's goodness, more clearly manifest. These blessings may be a direct address to God, used in "Blessed are You..." as in many of our prayers, or in the third person, "Blessed be God," or in popular modern form, *Baruch Hashem* (literally, "blessed is the Name").

Blessings on Mitzvot

Certain blessings include the phrase, *asher kid'shanu b'mitzvotav v'tzivanu*, "who has sanctified us with His commandments and commanded us . . ." These are specific acts commanded by the Torah or instituted by the rabbinic sages; examples include performing *brit milah* (circumcision), putting a *mezuzah* on the doorpost, blowing the shofar on Rosh Hashanah, lighting candles on Shabbat and holidays, washing hands before eating bread, reading the Book of Esther on Purim, and studying Torah.

In general, these blessings express our gratitude at being given specific commands that commission us to "call on the name of the Lord," i.e. to bring awareness of God into the world.

Blessings on Pleasures

Basic to Jewish theology is that the world is good, and enjoyment of God's creation gives us occasion for gratitude and praise. When we eat or drink, when we taste a new fruit of the season or don new clothes, this is an occasion for blessing. The sages of the Talmud say that while the altar atoned for us when the Temple stood, now, after the destruction, a person's table atones (Chagigah 27a). Saying blessings over food is a central Jewish form of worship.

The sages categorized food by types, encouraging us to appreciate the unique source of each food. Fruits from trees have a different blessing than vegetables from the ground, and those are different from grains. Animal-based foods have a different, more general blessing. A meal with bread takes the blessing *ha-motzi*, which also covers all food at the table. In addition, there are different after-blessings for different types of food, including special additions for the "seven species," certain fruits and grains grown in the Land of Israel.

The mystics explain further that the blessing we say before eating a food is to awaken the energies within the food. The blessing after eating is to awaken the energies within our bodies that enable us to digest the food. Both the diversity of blessings and the before/after "liturgy of the meal" (or even the snack) show a deep appreciation of the complex forces that sustain life in all its vitality.

In the Koren Siddur, you will find the blessings before and after food on pages 994-997; as well as *Bircat HaMazon*, said after a meal with bread, on pages 974-993.

Blessings on Remarkable Phenomena

In addition to the food and drink required to sustain us, living on this earth offers a multitude of experiences that can awaken our wonder. Our tradition created blessings for many of these - the first blossoming trees in the spring, the vast ocean, the experiences of thunder and lightning, the phenomena of humans with great wisdom, and many more. You can have a whole repertoire of blessings to enrich your life if you become familiar with the list in Koren-Sacks, page 999-1005, and refer to it often.

Blessings in the Prayer Service

Finally, as mentioned above, our prayer services are structured with blessings. In Talmudic times, a series of blessings was created around the ordinary events of getting up and preparing for one's day – these are now part of our Morning Blessings. The Verses of Song (*Pesukei d'Zimrah*, an Aramaic phrase) begin and end with a blessing on the phenomenon of song. The *Shema* is cradled by blessings, slightly different for morning and evening recitals of the *Shema*. And the "Standing" prayer or *Amidah*, so called because we stand up for it, and known on weekdays as the *Shemoneh esreh* or "18," is a fundamental statement of rabbinic Judaism itself, expressed as a series of blessings.

These blessings can become as familiar to you as the palm of your hand. They provide a map for the prayer services, and for your own daily spiritual enrichment. In the chapters that follow, we will study them in some depth.

How Blessings Shape Our Prayers

Blessings are used to create pattern or structure. When you understand this, you will be better able to follow each section of prayer. Some blessings, beyond their content, help create the drama of liturgy by offering stage instructions: open a scene, continue the scene, close a scene. Here are the major types of blessings from the point of view of their form:

Short Form Blessings are the simplest, as their name suggests. They are significant primarily for their content rather than as signals about the scene. They begin with the familiar formula: *Blessed are You, Adonai, Our God, King of the universe...*then end with a short statement of a characteristic of God, such as "Who frees the bound." Most of the blessings in *Birchot haShachar* are like this. Blessings over mitzvot, mentioned in the previous section, are also usually quite short. They add only the phrase "who has sanctified us with His commandments and commanded us to...," then mention the act that we are about to do, such as "hear the shofar."

Long Form Blessings begin with the same introductory formula (*petichah* or opening), but add a more elaborate statement about God or the acts that God has done in the world. With this kind of blessing, there will also be at the end a closing line, which uses a different version of the words blessing God, and generally refers back to the same theme as the opening of the blessing. For example, the blessing over creation of light, before the *Shema* (bottom of page 88), begins *Blessed are You, Adonai, Our God, King of the universe, Who forms light and creates darkness, makes peace and creates everything.* It continues with a lengthy intermediate section on the created lights and praises of angels, then concludes (bottom of page

94): *Blessed are You, Adonai, who creates the lights.* The theme is the same as the opening, namely light; but note the change from singular, "light," to plural, "lights".

Another example is the prayer of gratitude for our bodies, a long form blessing from the *Birchot haShachar* (page 4):

> Blessed are You, *Adonai*, Our God, King of the universe, Who has made the human being with wisdom, and created him with openings and cavities, so that if one of them were opened, or one of them were closed, we would not be able to stand before you.
> Blessed are You *Adonai*, who heals all flesh and does wonders.

Here again, the conclusion does not precisely repeat the words of the opening – making and creating – but amplifies them by describing God's action as healing and doing wonders.

The last line is called the *chatimah,* or "seal," of the long-form blessing. (The word *chatimah* may also be used for the last line(s) of a significant section of prayer, whether it is a blessing or not.)

Series Form Blessings are a collection of blessings that each have a *chatimah* or ending line, but only the first blessing begins with the formula "Blessed are You, *Adonai,* Our God, King of the universe." If you look at the daily *Amidah* starting on page 108 of the Koren Siddur, you will see an example. The first blessing begins with the usual formula and ends with "Blessed are You, *Adonai,* Shield of Abraham." You might expect, based on your experience of studying other blessings, that the second blessing would begin with the usual formula again (*Baruch ata, Adonai...*). But instead, it goes directly into a new topic that the blessing is concerned with, namely God's power over life and death: "You are mighty eternally..." (page 110) This topic ends with its particular *chatimah*, "Blessed are You *Adonai*, Who gives life to the dead." Thus the pattern continues, for the entire *Amidah*.

In a series blessing, it can sometimes be difficult to figure out where a new blessing begins. With the blessings before the morning *Shema*, for example, if you are told there are two blessings before the *Shema*, you might turn to that section (starting on page 88) and look for two places where you see the words, "Blessed are You, *Adonai*, Our God, King of the universe." But you would find only one. This is because the section uses the pattern of two long-form blessings in series, combining the two styles. You can, however, find two *chatimot*:

> Blessed are You, *Adonai*, Who creates the lights. (page 94)
> Blessed are You, *Adonai*, Who chooses His people Israel in love. (page 96)

You find the beginning of the second blessing by going to the paragraph immediately after the first *chatimah*, which here is the *Ahavah rabbah* prayer, "With great love you have loved us..."

When prayer services are more complex, such as on the High Holy Days, these structures help you find your way among the sections of prayer.[4]

The Architecture of Prayer: Mirroring Meaning

Our prayer books today are, unfortunately, books. I say "unfortunately" because books require a certain format that is somewhat inappropriate to prayer. Think of the difference between reading the script of a play and seeing it performed.

The mode of printing requires linear formatting, and the best one can do is arrange some of the text differently, as scriptwriters do. Similarly with our prayers; often the best we can do is arrange them as poetry and divide sections clearly. But this tells you nothing about the relationship between the segments through which you are traveling, or how the beginning relates to the end. In a novel, there is a plot structure, and you know the story will unfold if you keep going. You may even "peek ahead" if you get tired of reading, just to stay interested. But the novel is mostly linear, unless the author uses flashbacks or is interweaving multiple stories. Not so our prayers.

As a result, when using our books, we plod along through a prayer service as though it has no growth or dynamism at all. There will be some highlights, when the cantor sings a beautiful piece or the congregation chants together, but – so what? Maybe the sermon will be interesting...Maybe if I concentrate on this part that I like, I'll be inspired today...

Most of us, most of the time, are missing a major point. There is a significant structural piece that would change our experience dramatically if we were aware of it; if the music of the service played upon it; if we thought about it in retrospect or prospect. It is what Rabbi Sacks in his introduction to the Koren Siddur refers to as "mirror imaging," what literary critics term "chiasmus," and I will call – to give it a personal, physical referent – the "necklace."[5]

Earlier, we referred to the significance of the *koach ha-dimyon* (power of imagination) in prayer. Let's exercise that power by imagining that you are walking on a trail through the woods on an oval path, which takes you around a pond and then leads you back to the beginning. When you get to the farther end of the oval, there is a place to pause and sit for a moment.

And then, as you round the bend and start back, from the other side of the oval, you can see the same pond, the foliage around it, the trees on the other side; but from different perspectives so that they are uncannily the same and different. As you return to the trailhead, you look back over the terrain and can see more diversity and complexity than appeared at the beginning.

While there is a beginning and end to this trail, one's perspective is not linear like a story plot. If you said, "I saw X, then I saw Y, then I saw Z..." it would not begin to convey the experience of this walk on the oval trail. Nor is the end quite the same as the beginning even though you are at the same geographical spot.

A necklace because of its familiarity as a personal object can help us with this imagery. You, the wearer, are at the beginning and end, the "latch." The two sides match in length – although, in some necklaces, they might not be exactly symmetrical in decoration.

A pendant hangs at the opposite end of the oval; it provides a focus for attention. Depending on one's consciousness at any given time, one can pay attention to the symmetries, the view across the oval from one point to another, to the pendant or turn-around point, to the latch, or to the whole.

This structure appears in a surprising number of our prayers. In a miniature format, it can even be seen in a long-form blessing, between the *petichah* or beginning formula and the ending *chatimah*. The blessing we say in the morning thanking God for our bodies, which we looked at briefly above, is an example. In English, it goes as follows:

> Blessed are you, *Adonai* our God, king of the universe, who created the human with wisdom; and created many channels and openings. It is revealed and known before your Glory that if one of these were opened or one of these were closed [opposite to its intended function] it would be impossible to stand before you. Blessed are you, *Adonai*, who heals all flesh and does wonders.

This seems straightforward and easy to understand, but it contains a hidden complexity. The blessing starts with a simple statement about wisdom in the body. Think of a museum that is offering an exhibit on the human body and starts with a photo of a physically fit and balanced body. We perceive symmetry and beauty. Then, however, we are introduced to its "insides" and discover that it's much more complicated!

After walking through a few exhibits about the digestive, respiratory, and neurological system ("channels and openings"), we are advised how fragile this system is, such that we can be undermined at any moment by a small dysfunction. With that knowledge "revealed," we have a very different feeling from at the beginning: precisely because we now see its vulnerability ("it would be impossible to stand"), we recognize the body as a great treasure. The blessing closes, going beyond the obvious "wisdom" of the beginning and proclaiming God as a healer of all flesh and a worker of "wonders." And we say, Amen.

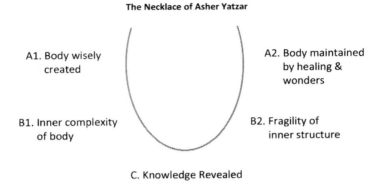

The Necklace of Asher Yatzar

A1. Body wisely
created

A2. Body maintained
by healing &
wonders

B1. Inner complexity
of body

B2. Fragility of
inner structure

C. Knowledge Revealed

The blessing has a subtle internal structure that registers primarily at an unconscious level, until we bring it out consciously and appreciate its message, which might be stated: the divine wisdom we see in the body is undergirded or accentuated by the divine power of healing.

As you can see above, I indicated the segments of the prayer with letters, following a convention often used in literary studies to analyze complex structures. If letter A represents a certain type of content, the variations on that content are A1, A2, A3.... Another kind of content would be represented by B, and its variations would be B1, B2, etc. For the prayer above, A would be the creation of the body, B would be the inner structure, and C would be the knowledge of it. The variations show us different aspects.

In the above, we would say the chiasmus structure is AB-CBA. For another prayer or set of prayers, we could use the letters to represent different items.

The necklace structure occurs many times in our prayers. We can see it even at the broad formal level of our four sections of prayer. As we saw above, there are four main sections of prayer:

1) Morning Blessings,
2) Verses of Song,
3) The *Shema* and Its Blessings, and
4) The *Amidah* (*Shemoneh esreh*).

(This is a good chance for you to flip through the service in the siddur and become more familiar with the sections and the terminology we used above.)

The core of the first section is primarily a group of short-form blessings. (See Koren, pp. 26-29).

The second section is a collection of biblical psalms and other chanted pieces, bookended by a long-form blessing at the beginning (pp. 62-65) and a long-form blessing at the end (pp. 82-85) which are in series form. Recall that in a series, the final blessing does not begin with the usual *Baruch ata...* formula, thereby showing that it is related to the first blessing. This is a series even if there are only two blessings.

The third section is a collection of biblical passages (=the *Shema* proper) bookended by two long-form series blessings at the beginning (pp. 88-97) and one long-form blessing at the end (pp. 102-107).

The fourth section, the *Amidah*, is a series of blessings (pp. 108-133) which are long-form with varying complexity. Since they are in a series, you can't find the beginning of a blessing by looking for *Baruch ata* (so it would be a good exercise for you to find the *chatimah* for each blessing).

Do you see a pattern?

Let's use "A" to designate a section made up of blessings only, and "B" to designate a section containing biblical passages bookended by long-form blessings. Then the structure of the four parts of the service is A-B-B-A:

A1 – Morning Blessings (many short-form blessings)

B1 – Verses of Song (blessing – biblical passages – blessing)

B2 – *Shema* and Blessings (2 blessings – biblical passages – blessing)

A2 – *Amidah* (series of many blessings)

Now let's ask, is there a center point where B1 and B2 meet? (Look on page 88 of Koren-Sacks.) Yes. This is the *Barchu*, the call to prayer, when the individuals become a community in prayer. So if C = *Barchu*, the structure is now ABCBA, and *Barchu* is the turning point of the necklace.

As Rabbi Sacks points out, these mirroring patterns represent the basic structure of the ancient literary figure of speech known as chiasmus.[6] They create "inverted parallelism," parallel in form or content but reversing their order (ABC becomes CBA), amplifying or accentuating the meaning by the slight differences in nuance between the first sequence and its reversal – as we have seen in miniature already.

We should note that there is a very common kind of parallelism in biblical literature and prayer where the content is not reversed; rather it is straightforward, A - B - A - B. For example,

A) Majesty and splendor are   B) before him,

A) Strength and beauty are   B) in His place. (p. 66)

The letter A represents attributes of God; B represents a location. The two lines are exactly parallel, reinforcing one another. With chiasmus, the order is switched. In the following, again A represents the attribute or possession; B represents the place:

B) In the heights of the universe is   A) your dwelling,

A) Your justice and rightness are   B) to the ends of
    the earth.(104)

Is there a big difference? Perhaps not as we read it from our usual conscious perspective; they are both elegant poetic features. But, on a deeper level, chiasmus provides closure. While straightforward parallelism has a forward movement - it can go on and on, with expansion as in ABABABAB..., chiasmus with its reversal brings us back to the beginning. There is an unconscious satisfaction in completing the circle. This is the oval of the path around the pond, or the oval of the necklace.

To review: for our study of the weekday morning liturgy, let us imagine the overall necklace structure as follows:

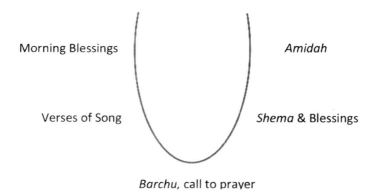

Morning Blessings   *Amidah*

Verses of Song   *Shema* & Blessings

Barchu, call to prayer

The mirror structure provides, and provokes us to contemplate, a relation between the blessings said privately at the beginning of the service, and the silent *Amidah* near the end. It also invites us to attend to the relation between the bookend blessings of the Verses of Song and those of the *Shema*; and the content of the biblical passages in each. At the same time, it brings us around in a circle to where we started - but with a richer and deeper experience.

Carrying the imaginative exploration further, what if the music or chants that we used highlighted these patterns? And, are there more? We will see indeed that there are necklaces within necklaces, mirrors within mirrors, in our prayers.

Gratitude: No Matter Too Small

Now that we are alert to the structure, we can circle back to the first section of prayers, the *Birchot ha-Shachar* or Morning Blessings, representing the world of *Asiyah*. The section in its entirety contains many items besides blessings. There are recitations from biblical passages, including the *Akedat Yitzchak* (binding of Isaac) and *korbanot* (sacrifices). A short version of the *Shema* appears in this section, along with supplementary prayers. But the core of this section is a long list of blessings.

We know from the Talmud that blessings were part of the normal routine of a person's arising, getting dressed, and preparing for the day ahead. In Judaism, simple daily acts such as these become religious acts when accompanied with God-consciousness, brought about by the recital of a blessing with God's name. They are ways of sanctifying the World of Action, the world of physicality, social roles, performance and goals.

After *Modeh* (*Modah* for women) *Ani*, the prayer on waking, we wash hands and say a blessing. We say blessings over the body, soul, and Torah study, as well as blessings over putting on *tallit* and *tefillin* if you wear them.[7] The blessings over body and soul are series blessings, both long-form (Koren pages 4-5).

We considered the blessing over the body earlier ("You created the human being with wisdom..."). The blessing over the soul, which begins with the words *Elohai neshamah*, continues immediately without the usual formula, so is in series with the blessing over on the body.

> My God, the soul you placed within me is pure. You created it, You formed it, You breathed it into me, and You guard it while it is within me, and in the future You will take it from me and restore it to me in the future to come. All the time that the soul is within me, I thank You, Adonai my God and the God of my ancestors, Master of all works, Lord of all souls. Blessed are You, Adonai, who restores souls to lifeless bodies.

This blessing resonates directly with our study because it alludes to the four worlds in terms of levels of soul: the pure soul (*Atzilut*), creating (*Beriah*), forming (*Yetzirah*), and breathing it into the physical body (*Asiyah*). Moreover, as you can see below, it has its own "necklace" structure:

- In the left column, the original purity of the soul alludes to the world of *Atzilut.*
- The terms *bara* and *yatzar* correlate with the worlds *Beriah* and *Yetzirah.*
- "You breathed it into me" grounds the soul in the world of *Asiyah,* which is alluded to also in the right-hand column by calling God "Master of all deeds" (Rabbi Sacks translates it as "works"), using the same root as *Asiyah.*
- The three levels of God's creation of the soul and infusion of it into a body are reflected, across the necklace, by the phrase "Master of deeds,"
- While the phrase "soul is pure" parallels the appellation "Lord of all souls."
- The two present-life references, "You guard it" and "I thank you" express the soul's relation to God while in the body.
- The "midpoint" of the meaning of the prayer, what God will do in the future to "me," parallels the *chatimah,* affirming that God restores life to all.
- The phrase of address, "Lord my God and God of my ancestors," is not exactly in order across the necklace from the first address to God, but clearly relates to it, amplifying the prayer from the personal to the collective.

Isn't it remarkable that such a short prayer can have this complex structure?

The blessings over Torah study are comparatively much simpler and do not use chiasmus. Briefly, they are as follows:

Blessed are You, *Adonai* our God, King of the Universe, who has sanctified us with your commandments and commanded us to occupy ourselves with words of Torah.

That is a short-form commandment over a *mitzvah*. It is followed by a long-form blessing, but without the opening formula, indicating that these are a connected series:

> Please make the words of Torah sweet, *Adonai* our God and God of our ancestors, in our mouth and in the mouths of all your people, the Family of Israel. And may it be that we, our descendants and the descendants of Your people the Family of Israel, all of us, will know Your name and study Your Torah for its own sake. Blessed are You, *Adonai*, who teaches Torah to His people Israel.

A final blessing over Torah, with an opening and a *chatimah*, is the same that is said when a person is called to the Torah in a public service:

> Blessed are You, *Adonai* our God, King of the universe, who chose us from all peoples and gave us the Torah. Blessed are You, *Adonai*, who gives the Torah.

We follow this by reciting passages from the written Torah and oral Torah (Mishnah and Gemara), so that the blessing is followed by the act that was commanded in the first blessing. As mentioned earlier, those who wear a *tallit* (prayer shawl with *tzitzit*, fringes) and *tefillin* (head and hand ornaments) then don them, with their accompanying blessings over the mitzvot, in preparation for formal prayer.

The remaining blessings in *Birchot HaShachar* make powerful statements about God's concern for every detail of our being. On the physical level, each vessel and sinew of our body is of Divine concern; on the spiritual level, the soul is tended while we sleep and it is as if we were recreated each morning.

The practice of saying blessings as we go through each gesture of the morning is itself a testimony to the care and concern that Jews have felt from God, and their recognition that everything comes from the help that is constantly provided.

Most of the blessings are taken almost verbatim from the Talmudic tractate Berachot (60b). You can find in the Talmud the corresponding blessings to the ones in Koren-Sacks, pages 26-30, as well as some of the ones mentioned above.[8] The blessings over Torah study appear in Berachot 11b. In all of them, the differences between our version and the Talmud's, some 1500 or more years ago, are negligible. We can imagine people in the ancient stone houses of Babylonia or Israel getting up and reciting the same phrases we do today. Although they were said in the privacy of one's home, with a blessing corresponding to each act, the practice created a sense of connection to the larger community, because it was what everyone did.

Today, we also say these blessings quickly at the beginning of morning services. The intent is to enable people who may have forgotten or been in too much of a hurry to say them at home, to satisfy their obligation by saying "Amen" to the prayer leader's recital. This custom probably began in the Middle Ages and, as they were formalized, different communities created a different order for the prayers.

The list in the Talmud page cited above does not include three "negative blessings" -for not making me a non-Jew, a slave, or a woman. Those are in a different tractate of the Talmud. Modern denominations, except for the orthodox, have changed these blessings to a positive form, and even the orthodox for centuries have had a different blessing for women to say. Apart from the fact that the statements appear arrogant to the modern reader, they are also the only blessings that are negative. This seems to contradict the whole purpose of blessing, which, you will recall, is to draw out the unfulfilled potential of the person or thing being blessed. We wouldn't take a pear and say, "Blessed are You...for not making this an apple." However, as part of our tradition, we can see these as essentially blessings relating to the social and religious status of the person.

The total number of positive blessings, counting three blessings over the Torah, is eighteen. This is very close to the number in the *Amidah*, suggesting that, as we mentioned in the last section, the compilers of the morning blessings thought of these as parallel to the *Amidah*. This leads us to ask whether there is an internal structure to the blessings as we have them now. Indeed there seems to be.

Remember that this is the World of *Asiyah*, the world of physicality, social roles, and action. Leaving out the three negative blessings, we can note that most of the blessings[9] engage our attention on different parts of the body:

Ability to tell day from night	Brain
Opens eyes of blind	Eyes
Clothes the naked	Torso
Frees the bound	Arms
Raises the bowed	Back and knees
Spreads earth over waters	Feet, on the ground
Provides all my needs	Shoes (see Talmud)
Makes firm the steps	Feet, walking
Girds with strength	Torso
Crowns with glory	Head
Gives strength to weary	All
Removes sleep from eyes, slumber from eyelids	Eyes
Keep me close to good, far from evil	Moral being, psyche

While the order is not perfect, it seems as though the list is intended to go from head to foot, pausing at the earth/waters juncture, and then return upward again. If we were to describe this as a necklace, it might look like the diagram below. Notice how the two sides mirror each other not-exactly, provoking us to think about their similarities and differences.

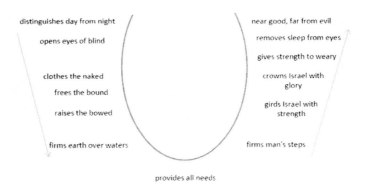

The necklace of Birchot HaShachar

distinguishes day from night

opens eyes of blind

clothes the naked

frees the bound

raises the bowed

firms earth over waters

near good, far from evil

removes sleep from eyes

gives strength to weary

crowns Israel with glory

girds Israel with strength

firms man's steps

provides all needs

In the above schema, the parallels are striking. "Gives strength to the weary" near the end (third from top on right side) seems out of place and perhaps redundant to "girds Israel with strength," but other aspects match very well, even to the firm earth over the waters being parallel to "firming" one's steps.

Judaism did not develop a "yoga," in the sense of a formalized body-prayer. But since the morning *brachot* were intended to be said as one went through the natural body movements of arising, orienting oneself, getting dressed, and centering one's moral self, they offer a framework for regular practice. With attention and intention – *kavannah* – the morning *brachot* can become that "yoke" (the root meaning of yoga) or discipline. We have the opportunity to choreograph our own personal prayers.

Most of all, we have the opportunity with *Birchot Ha-Shachar* to practice gratitude. Nothing is too small for God's concern, and nothing too small for our thanks and appreciation - for being alive, for the abilities we have to move, see, speak, learn, and nourish our spirits, for sleep and waking, for awareness and moral imagination.

Chapter 3

Songs of Life

The second portion of morning prayers, *Pesukei d'Zimrah* or "Verses of Song," introduces us to the second of the Four Worlds – *Yetzirah*, the World of Formation. As we noted in the first chapter, this world points to tendencies or felt direction. While it is also associated with emotions, we use that term to mean the currents that give shape to our reality, behind the scenes of our visible, tangible, audible actions. Temperament, ranges of sensitivity and receptivity, intangible influences are all part of this world.

Our psychological reality is such that we often are not receptive to the currents beyond our own limited reality. We experience many emotional reactions that are basically versions of pleasure versus pain; and, as with physical sensations, we seek the first and avoid the second. We are often invested in ego-emotions that replicate the approach-avoidance reaction on the level of the psyche, that is, how the ego feels. We "feel insulted," for example, or we are pleased by praise. On any given day, these can occupy a great deal of our attention, especially the painful ones. They lead us into defensive, alienated postures in relation to others. And if we walk around "feeling defensive," we actually are not feeling much at all.

This is the challenge of the world of Formation. In the World of Action we are corrupted by an overemphasis on goals, accomplishments, and "doing," so that we have a constant need to control. In the World of Formation, our psyche is corrupted

by defensiveness and fear. A *tikun* for our overly-controlling
ego was gratitude and humility; hence the morning blessings.
Clearly, a correction for defensiveness would be openness
and connectedness – but, when one is feeling defensive and
isolated, that very openness can seem fearful. But there is a
universal and consistently helpful method for generating expanded emotional connection – namely, music. Song, melody,
chant, rhythm, instrumental music; also the verbal music of
poetry and the physical rhythm of dance can all generate a
larger sense of connectedness and can lead to expanded states
of consciousness.

Our sages knew that music and chant can set the tone
for a world of feelings, and this was the implicit purpose of
Pesukei d'Zimrah. Building on an older custom of chanting *Tehillim* (Psalms), they crafted a section of prayer that was designed to induce a joyful and even exalted atmosphere inside
and out. This was not a new invention; virtually every religious
and spiritual tradition does this, each in its own way, creating
an energy to supplement or even evoke certain states of feeling
and energy.

For the purpose of creating community, examples are
meditative tones played by instruments, or energetic drum-
ming and chanting to induce trance. Solemn music accompanies certain kinds of ceremonies; other rituals create community by group singing or chanting. Our tradition created an
interlude for music knowing that it was helpful both in building community and in preparing for inspiration – that is, for
being receptive to God. An exhilarated, anticipatory state of
consciousness prepares us for an encounter with the divine.[10]

As a scene in our drama, this world also has a star person-
age: King David. We will see later how as author of psalms he

represents the passion of life and a great love of God. Together with the Temple, which was his unfulfilled dream, the presence of David the poet-king infuses this entire section. The rabbis also had a tradition that the celebrations of Jews coming to the Temple in Jerusalem provided the greatest experiences of joy, particularly at the pilgrimage festivals and, among those, even more at the fall festival, the Sukkot holiday. Living centuries after the destruction of the Temple, our teachers brought together biblical passages relating to Temple traditions to awaken joy and energize the people in their own days.

Imagining Joy

As the name clearly says, our *Pesukei d'Zimrah* is a collection of segments (*posuk* means "verse") of song. At some point, a liturgist (or a group) gathered together some of the more widely known and used biblical passages, chants, recitals, and songs, and framed them between two blessings. Just as Rabban Gamliel had known that in the era after the destruction of the Temple the community needed a fixed prayer (see chapter 5), at some point in the Talmudic period it became clear that people needed an organized session of song – perhaps similar to the way congregations feel the need for a choir today – to set the tone for prayer. Rabbi Elie Munk, the former chief rabbi of France, wrote that "the worshipper does not always find himself in the proper mood to join in the joyous theme-song of the cosmos," so the songs themselves encourage him.[11]

The psalms and other biblical selections, as well as the rabbinic prayers in this section, are clearly meant to create an environment of high energy and happiness. "Halleluyah!", which echoes through the main part of the prayer, is a shout of praise and exultation. As the syllables suggest, it is like the ululation of voices celebrating a wedding or a victory. Thus, by the time a congregation reaches the final blessing of the section, *Yishta-bach*, they can be in a state of happiness from the music, chanting, and inspiring words of the songs.

Most congregations have only a slice of this feeling today. While the songs were to be chanted or sung, the original melodies are not known, and the few chant tropes handed down to us do not often resonate with our modern musical senses. The small repertoire of music in common use for this section of prayer, particularly on weekdays, usually includes a few melodies such as for Psalm 150 and the trope for the Song of the Sea. Even in traditional congregations where these songs and prayers are recited in full, they are usually quickly mumbled by members of the congregation.

So, again, we must use our imaginations. Neurobiologists tell us that imagining something can activate the same neuronal responses as actually having it in physical reality. Imagining a delicious crisp apple in our mind can initiate salivation; imagining a roller coaster ride can trigger a sharp intake of breath. We can imagine song as well. Of course, we can sing to ourselves; but we can imagine a chorus even if we are alone. Imagination that can generate positive emotions, improving our ability to experience and express happiness, helps to establish a foundation of health.

Music can "re-set" our emotional frame, which is tested daily by all kinds of stress. From ancient times, the joy of life found expression in poetry and song, and communal participation in that expression often added an intensity that elevated and expanded each person's joy. The framers of *Pesukei d'Zimrah* must have intended something along those lines. The more we understand that, the easier it will be for us to reinvent a world of sound, vibration, melody and rhythm that will benefit our communities.

David, the Heroic Poet

In this World of *Yetzirah*, the main character is David the poet and visionary, and his memory is invoked many times to set the tone for our worship. While known historically as David HaMelech, the great king who united the tribes and established a capital in Jerusalem, he is beloved by the Jewish people as a master of the expression of human feeling. He combined a deep humanity – including human desire and pride as well as courage – with a great devotion to God, both of which he expressed in his poetry.

Most of the book of Psalms is traditionally attributed to King David, who became king of the united people of Israel around 1000 B.C.E. and reigned for forty years. We have no reason to doubt that David was musically and poetically talented; but whether he wrote all the hymns that are connected with his name is open to question. It was common in ancient times to write a poem in honor of someone and affix his name to it; or there may have been a "school" of Davidic poetry. Nevertheless, the popular poems that address David's struggles and victories became a model for the Jewish people. He could declare love and contentment with God despite the challenges of life. One cannot help but be moved by David's "one thing I ask, to live in the house of God," or "even though I walk through the valley of the shadow of death, I fear no evil; for You are with me." This faith and yearning have inspired thousands of people for generations.

David thus is the poet of faith, and heralds the songs and chants of our morning service. Psalm 30, "for the dedication of Your house," is a paean to God who recreates us each morning so that the soul can sing:

> At night there may be weeping, but in the morning there is joy...You have turned my mourning into dancing; You have removed my sackcloth and clothed me with joy, so that my soul may sing to You and not be silent.

He is invoked in *Baruch She'amar*, the blessing that opens the *Pesukei d'Zimrah* (p. 64 in Koren):

> . . .With the songs of Your servant David we will praise You, O *Adonai* our God...Blessed are You, *Adonai*, the King extolled with songs of praise.

Following this is *Hodu*, a psalm from the book *Divrei ha-Yamim* (Chronicles), to celebrate the bringing of the Ark of the Covenant to Jerusalem (pp. 65-66). This most glorious moment is described in the book of Samuel:

> *And David and all the house of Israel played before the Lord with all manner of instruments made of cypress-wood, and with harps, and with psalteries, and with timbrels, and with sistra, and with cymbals... And David danced before the Lord with all his might; and David was girded with a linen ephod; and David and all the house of Israel brought up the ark of the Lord with shouting, and with the sound of the horn. (2 Samuel 6: 5, 14-15)*

In the city that David had made his capital, unity between God and the people was at hand -- a unique time of glory and harmony. We echo it with the *Hodu*:

> Give thanks unto *Adonai*, call His name! Make known among the peoples His acts! Sing to Him, chant to Him; tell of all His marvels! Make praises in His holy name -- may the heart rejoice of those who seek *Adonai*.

The story in Chronicles tells us that on that day David created a regular choir and orchestra: he ordained "Asaph and his kinsmen," that is, a group of Levites under a chief conductor, for the ceremonies of thanks to God.

David is also celebrated as the author of the favored psalm 145. This psalm appears three times in our daily prayers, twice in *shacharit* and once in *mincha*. (The rabbis said that a person who recites this prayer three times a day has earned a place in the world to come.) Its twenty-one verses are said to reflect the name of God at the burning bush, *Ehyeh asher ehyeh*, as the word *ehyeh* ("I will be") has the numerological value of 21, thus mystically connecting David to Moses.[12] "Every day I will bless You!" he exclaims.

David appears again after the recital of the six psalms that end the book of Psalms, giving thanks at the end of his life for having been able to gather the resources he would pass on to Solomon, his son, to build the Temple in Jerusalem. The story is told in 1 Chronicles 29 (and we will examine this passage further below).

The siddur thus invites us to sing with David in these psalms, as the figure of David points the way to communion with God. He teaches us that our soul wants to sing and not be silent. We acclaim God by singing David's songs; we recite his prayer over the Ark of the Covenant, symbolizing God's revelation to the Jewish people; and we recite his prayer thanking God for the resources to build the Temple. David shows not only how to sing praises to God, but also, by alluding to the Ark and the Temple, emphasizes our potential for bringing God's presence to life among the Jewish people.

Happy Are Those Who Dwell in Your House

King David's desire was to build the Temple of God, but he was not allowed to do so.[13] Yet his passion reminds us of an aspect of our worship that is behind the scenes. David looked forward to the Temple; the sages looked backward and longed for it. Why? It is very difficult for moderns to understand, as we tend to think of the Temple as a place of ritual and sacrifice, and of the critiques mounted against it by Christians in their scriptures. But in the deeper understanding of ancient Israel, the Temple was actually a primary symbol of life.

Jon Levenson, in his book *Resurrection and the Restoration of Israel: The Ultimate Victory of the God of Life*, convincingly demonstrates that the Temple was the antipode of Sheol, that is, the opposite place in Israelite cosmology of the realm of death. Not all who died went to Sheol, but that place was particularly associated with dying an unhappy death, outside the blessing of God.

The verse quoted above that opens *Ashrei*, "Happy are those who dwell in your House!" indicates the joy imagined in the Temple. The psalmist's wish "may I dwell in your House for many long years" (Psalms 23:6) expresses the belief that it is a life-enhancing place. Some translate the expression *l'orech yamim*, literally "for length of days," as "forever," suggesting eternal life. The priestly blessing chanted in the Temple over the assembled crowds included a blessing for life: "May the Lord bless and preserve you..." According to a midrash, the spring gushing from under the Temple was connected to the Garden of Eden. As king, Solomon enhanced the Temple's image as a place of vitality and nourishment by furnishing the temple with exotic plants and trees as imagery of life. In short, while not promising immortality, the Temple guarded, nourished and lengthened life.

The Temple was also the place of epiphany, of the revelation of God's glory. Sacrifices were more than expressions of gratitude and meals for the devotees and priests; they were also ritual spaces for revelation. In the time of the dedication of the *Mishkan*, the desert tabernacle, after the first sacrifices were completed, "there appeared the Glory of the Lord to all the people" (Leviticus 9:23). Isaiah saw visions in the Temple. As Moses had assured the people even when they were afraid of the Divine presence, "You who cling to the Lord your God are all alive today" (Deuteronomy 4.4).

Thus Psalm 30, which makes the transition from the morning blessings to the Verses of Song, is entitled "A song for the dedication of the House," implying the Temple which was yet to be built. This invites us to imagine the first day on which the shining new building was opened in great ceremony.

We go back even further. The piece known as *Hodu* (by its first word, Koren pp. 64-67) embraces selections from *Divrei HaYamim* or Chronicles. As noted above, King David sang this at the bringing of the Ark of the Covenant to Jerusalem; tradition says that later, it was recited at the Temple in two parts, the first part at the morning sacrifices and the second at the evening ones.

Then we move to a song of personal offering. *Mizmor l'Todah*, Song of Thanksgiving (p. 70) is a distinctive psalm that recalls the thanksgiving offering brought to the Temple after having passed through a great danger.[14] Some congregations today stand for this prayer. Spiritually it represents a thanksgiving for all those times when we escaped danger and did not even know it, thus affirming the hidden miracles of our daily lives.

The next collection, *Y'hi k'vod* (pp. 70-71), is known primarily for the fact that it includes God's name twenty-one times.[15] But it alludes to the Temple as well. It begins with the verse, "May the Glory of the Lord be forever! May the Lord rejoice in His works!" As we noted above, the "glory of God" appeared when the sacrificial fire was offered at the ceremonies inaugurating the *Mishkan*, the desert tabernacle: "there appeared the glory of the Lord; and there came fire from before the Lord." The verse is telling us that the glory and the fire are a manifestation of God's rejoicing -- rejoicing in the *Mishkan* built by His people, which was itself a mirror of creation.[16] "May the Lord rejoice in His works!" Another verse in *Y'hi k'vod* shows the creation responding with joy: *Yismechu ha-shamayim v'tagel ha-aretz*, "May the heavens rejoice and the earth be glad!" Interestingly, the first letters of those four words form an acronym of God's name.

Thus the sequence, from the psalm of the dedication of the Temple through the collection *Y'hi k'vod*, expresses the greatness of the ceremonies of the Temple, the generative place of the richness of life, as well as divine joy and its reflection in creation. *Ashrei* and the five psalms that follow – the culmination of the book of psalms, 145 through 150 – are the people's response.

One helpful way of approaching this next set of psalms is to imagine them as part of a processional liturgy to the Temple. Psalm 145 emphasizes the "telling" or "proclaiming" of God's greatness and goodness, moving from an individual praising God to universal praise.[17] Psalm 146 follows up on some of its themes, first mentioning God the Creator, "Who made heaven and earth, the sea and all they contain." This makes specific some of God's "awesome deeds." It echoes the theme of benevolence of God: "He keeps faith forever...secures justice for the oppressed...gives food to the hungry...sets captives free...gives sight to the blind...raises those bowed down...loves the righteous...protects the stranger... gives courage to the orphan and widow."

Psalm 147 elaborates further, naming the good that God does for Israel on the one hand, and God's power over creation on the other. God "rebuilds Jerusalem...gathers the scattered exiles...heals the brokenhearted and binds up their wounds." His greatness as creator and sustainer of the world appears when he "counts the number of stars...covers the sky with clouds... provides the earth with rain...spreads snow like fleece...sprinkles frost like ashes...makes the wind blow and the waters flow." These themes alternate with one another throughout the poem, ending with "He has declared his words to Jacob, His statues and laws to Israel -- not for every nation..."

Psalm 148 shifts away from description toward exhortation to praise. The previous two psalms have mentioned singing - "I will sing" once in 146, "It is good to sing," "sing and make music," "sing" three times in 147. But now sounds breaks forth in force. The root *hallel*, praise, occurs repeatedly. All are exhorted to praise God - the heavens, angels, hosts, sun, moon and stars; the earth, sea monsters, seas, fire, hail, snow, mist, winds, mountains, trees, wild animals and domestic, crawling things, birds, kings, princes, judges, young and old, men and women. The psalm portrays a universal choir. And, at the end, the theme of the people of Israel comes forward, as the "people close to him."

Psalm 149 elaborates on the music. "Sing to the Lord a new song." Dancing, instruments like timbrel and harp are invited. The imagery becomes more vivid – "let them sing for joy on their beds; let high praises of God be in their throats" – and as the warriors are added to the chorus: "Exaltations of God are in their mouth, and a two-edged sword in their hand."

Finally, Psalm 150 brings in the whole orchestra: shofar, harp, lyre, timbrel, strings, flute, clashing and resounding cymbals, as well as dancing. The concert that is truly a culmination to the increase of praise – and the *hallel* root occurs more often than in any previous psalm.

From general praise we have moved to the appreciation of the details of the universe and specific blessings we enjoy. From speech, narrative, telling the story of God, as creator and redeemer of the weak and powerless, benefactor of Israel, we have grown to a symphony. Beginning with the single psalmist in 145 acclaiming the divine king, we now have heard the entire created universe responding in praise. The crescendo effect is tremendous. Reading the words in Hebrew, with the repeated breath of "*Ha--ah*" and the ululation of "*lelu*," the physical experience corresponds to the excitement of the words, as the movement of the tongue echoes the breath. And the final phrase, "Let all that breathes praise the Lord!" embodies the command for complete integration of the physical with the verbal and the musical.

If God came down in a cloud of glory, rejoicing, with fire, now praise from the people goes up in a cloud of song, with the breath of their life, the soul released from silence.

Sadly, we don't have a rich sense of the whole experience on which this is based, being at the Temple, seeing its ceremonies and hearing its music. Our experience of large groups of people getting together and singing includes concerts, raves, some processionals and parades. Rarely outside the synagogue do we experience even hearing others sing with a sense of holiness. In some communities, a community choir or professional choir helps. Rosh Hashanah and Yom Kippur sometimes provide the vertical dimension described here – glory descending and our songs ascending.

We need to use the power of our imaginations when we don't have the reality before us. An example comes from Rav Kook – Abraham Isaac Kook, the first chief rabbi of Palestine (d. 1935), a remarkable scholar and mystic. He was a *kohen* himself. In one of his books about Israel, he is writing about a *mitzvah* one does in the Land, the *mitzvah* of *ma'aser*, tithing. He is explaining that we don't have the concrete foundations on which these and other mitzvot of the land are constructed, but we can still do certain things --- and then, he suddenly experiences a vision. He writes:

Behold this vision appears before us and we are filled with a spirit of song exalted as the flight of eagles, in view of the light of the happy days that await our nation on our blessed soil: here is the Temple on its foundation, a pride and honor for all the nations and kingdoms, and here we carry with joy sheaves of our Land of Delight. We come with a spirit full of true freedom and pure trust to the silo and winery, full of grain and wine, and our heart is gladdened by the abundance of a Land of Delight. There appear before us priests, holy men, servants of the Temple of the Lord, God of Israel. Their hearts are full of love and kindness, the holy spirit floods their faces, and we recall the crescendo of holy feelings that filled us at the time we saw their faces, when we went up on pilgrimage; when we saw them standing to serve within our Temple, pride of our strength and delight of our eyes. How handsome and pleasant they are to us, and now here is our silo full of the blessing of the Lord from this Land of Delight that we inherited from our fathers, and the portions of these men, men of spirit, are with us. We are happy to give to them their tithes; we find within our midst an exalted feeling and rise together with the tithe to the spiritual niveau where these holy men ascend. Our soul is drenched with the bounty of heaven. And behold the Levites, these delicate ones who captivated our hearts with their harmonious music in the holy place during the festival, when we went up to see the glorious Temple of God in Jerusalem, to behold the face of the Master, Lord, God of Israel. Their joyous, delicate faces remind us of their holy music; we float in streams of spiritual joy and give them with a happy heart their portion, the tithe. Soon we will once again meet on the Mountain of God at the next festival. How proud we will be to see these kohanim and Levites of God at their holy work and music! Happy the people who has this; happy the people whose God is the Lord.

We, like Rav Kook, have to build our own context. The words and songs and chants were to bring the people to joy, and so we have to build, inwardly and in community, a sense of joy, so we can make a 'joyful noise unto the Lord.'

Reprise: the Temple

The section of glorious song ends with what appears to be a responsive blessing, although congregations rarely read it this way today:

Blessed be *Adonai* forever.
                    Amen and Amen.
Blessed be *Adonai* from Zion, dwelling in Jerusalem.
                    Halleluyah!
Blessed be *Adonai* God, God of Israel, who alone does wonders;
and blessed be the name of His glory forever, and may His glory fill the whole earth.
                    Amen and Amen.

Except, surprisingly, this is not the end. *Pesukei d'Zimrah* continues with a set of scriptural quotations from Chronicles and Nehemiah. First comes a blessing offered by David proclaiming that everything belongs to God:

Blessed are You, *Adonai*, God of our father Yisrael, forever and ever. Yours, *Adonai*, are the greatness and the power, and the glory and majesty and splendor, for everything in heaven and earth is yours. Yours, *Adonai*, is the kingdom; You are exalted as head over all. Both riches and honor are from You, and You reign over all; and in Your hand are power and strength, and it is in Your hand to make great and give strength to all. And so, our God, we thank you and give praise to Your glorious name. (p. 78)

At this point, in many traditional congregations, people donate to charity by putting coins in a *tzedaka* box. It seems likely that this is an old custom, as it fits perfectly with David's words of acknowledgment that all wealth is from God. Indeed, in the scriptural source, the quotation emphasizes the point:

> *And so who am I, and who are my people, that we gather the strength to bring an offering like this? All things are from You, and from Your own hand we have given to You. (1 Chronicles 29: 14)*[18]

In other words, this is the liturgical moment to give to charity or make a commitment to do so.

The biblical passages continue with a historical account from Nehemiah, who was the governor of Israel (appointed by the Persian king Artaxerxes) in the mid-fifth century B.C.E., at the same time as Ezra the Scribe was leading a renewal of Jewish life in the land. Nehemiah oversaw the rebuilding of the city and completion of the Second Temple. The dedication ceremonies began with a reading of the Torah by Ezra to the whole people on Rosh Hashanah. The people wept – but Nehemiah and Ezra told them not to weep, for it was a holy day to rejoice. The holiday of Sukkot would soon follow, and they were to celebrate that with joy as well. On the 24th of the month, however, a fast day was declared, and the Levites led a renewal ceremony of the covenant, reciting a history of the people's relationship to God, after which the people promised allegiance and pledged their donations to the support of the Temple.

Only the beginning of that account is in our prayers: it moves from creation – "You alone are the Lord; You made the heavens…" -- to the covenant with Abraham promising the Land, and then to the redemption from Egypt. At that point, the service turns to the Song of the Sea from the book of Exodus.

The Nehemiah passage alludes, for those who recognize the biblical context, to the larger context of a covenant renewal, repentance, and restoration of a relationship to God. But it can also be read simply as a preface to the Song of the Sea, which describes the liberation from Egypt but also, notably, ends with a reference to the Temple:

> You will bring them and plant them on the mountain of Your heritage —
> the place, Adonai, You made for Your dwelling,
> the Sanctuary, Adonai, Your hands established.
> Adonai will reign forever. (p.82)

A few additional verses from the prophets follow, accentuating the kingship of God and proclaiming for the future, "saviors will go up to Mount Zion" (Obadiah 1) and "on that day the Lord shall be One and His name One" (Zechariah 14). So this coda to *Pesukei d'Zimrah* points to a future culmination, suggesting the shape (*yetzirah*) of things to come. From there, we move to the closing blessing of the entire section.

The Framework of Pesukei d'Zimrah

After capturing the emotional sense of this whole section, let's return to the blessings that bookend the psalms, which convey an additional message.

The opening *brachah*, *Baruch She'amar*, is a chant of parallel phrases in praise of God.

Blessed is He
who spoke and the world existed. Blessed is He (response)[19]
　　[He] acts in the beginning
speaks and acts
decrees and fulfills
　　shows mercy on the earth
　　shows mercy to all creatures
　　fulfills a good reward to those who fear Him
lives forever and exists to eternity
redeems and saves. Blessed is His name (response)

While beginning with creation, the opening prayer proclaims that Divine providence continues. That is, God not only acted in the beginning but continues to fulfill decrees and promises, including ultimate redemption and salvation. It is said that among the devout congregations of medieval Germany, an hour would be devoted to chanting and meditating on this poem.

The structure is a creative use of parallels: the alternation of groups of lines with two verbs describing God's attributes, then longer lines with one verb. This creates repetition and rhythm with variation. We will see again this paired-attribute pattern.

The long-form blessing after the chant sets out the purpose of the *Pesukei d'Zimrah*, namely to praise God:

Blessed are You, *Adonai* our God, King of the universe, the God, the compassionate Father, the One extolled by the mouth of His people, praised and glorified by the tongue of His devoted ones and His servants.
With the songs of David Your servant we will praise You, *Adonai* our God,
With praises and songs we will magnify and praise You, glorify You, speak Your Name and proclaim Your kingship -- our King, our God, the One, Life of the Worlds, King, praised and glorified to all eternity [by] His great name.
Blessed are You, *Adonai*, King extolled with praises.

The emphasis is on God's kingship, acclaimed by "the mouth of His people...the tongue of His devoted ones and servants" using the "songs of David Your servant." But a unique phrase also appears: .., *the only One,* **Life of the Worlds.** Theologically, it conveys the idea of God's immanence and eternity, even while the expression "king" connotes transcendence. As Rabbi Munk suggests, this phrase describes God as the "constant living Source of all activity, . . dispensing life to all the worlds."[20]

Yishtabach, the concluding prayer and blessing of the *Pesukei d'Zimrah* (p. 84/85), is recited to close the section. Expressing the wish that God the King will be praised forever, it does not begin with a *Baruch ata*...but has a *chatimah,* thus suggesting that it is a continuation of a "series" blessing begun with *Baruch She'amar.* As with *Baruch She'amar* at the beginning, we find a list of words of acclamation. The flavor of the Hebrew is difficult to capture because English does not have many helpful words to translate "praise" and "song," whereas in contrast the rich Hebrew vocabulary for song tells us how important song was to the Jewish people in ancient times.[21]

May your name be praised forever, our King, the God, the King great and holy in heaven and on earth!
For to You these are fitting, *Adonai* our God and God of our ancestors:
song and praise
exultation and melody
strength and dominion
     eternity, greatness and power
praise and glory
holiness and kingship
blessings and thanks
     from now and till forever.

Blessed are You, *Adonai*, God, King, great in praises,
God of thanksgivings, Master of wonders, who delights
in melodic songs, King, God, Life of the worlds.

Note the structure: three pairs, then a triad, then three
pairs, totaling fifteen. The variable 3x2 / 1x3 /3x2 structure
offers repetition and variation, as in *Baruch She'amar*. We see
the paired-element pattern again. The lists here are nearly the
same length. The number of pairs, fifteen, is the numerical value of the first two letters of God's name, *yud* and *heh*, which
as the word "*Yah*" represent another name of God.[22] Fifteen
is also the number of steps leading up to the Temple, where
the Levites stood singing – an appropriate transition from the
Verses of Song and temple processionals to the visionary dimensions of the next section.

The final blessing of this section speaks of God as King exalted in praises, as with the opening blessing, but adds "God of
thanksgivings, Master of wonders." As we have seen before, the
chatimah amplifies on the original concept, in this case on the
God of providential care. Further, where the opening blessing
spoke of humans singing the songs of David, this blessing sees
God as he "who delights in melodic songs (*shirei zimrah*)," or as
we might say idiomatically, songs beyond song. Then the blessing
repeats the same unusual expression we saw in the *chatimah* of
Baruch She'amar: chei ha-olamim, "Life of the Worlds." The composer emphasizes the connection between the vitality of song and
the source of life: The Life of the Worlds delights in song.

With this phrase ringing in our ears, we are called to appreciate the life of music and the liveliness that is in song. All
the components of song – lyrics, rhythm, melody – have the

potential to regenerate our lives. In particular, as a *tikkun* from the world of *Yetzirah*, they have the power to move us emotionally, to direct our inclination (*yetzer*) toward the celebration of life, toward companionship with our fellow Jews, other humans, and the world we live in; and even, perhaps, to set our hearts on fire for God!

Now we can summarize the structure of *Pesukei d'Zimrah*. It has the general form of chiasmus, but it has two endings – one after Psalm 150, and one at *Yishtabach*. (It is not clear exactly when edits like this were made, except that we know the Song of the Sea was not included in all traditions as late as the eleventh or twelfth centuries. Some orders of prayer place it after *Yishtabach*.) Here is an outline of the section:

Preface: 1. Psalm 30 for dedication of the Temple
A1 - **Introduction: Baruch She'amar with long-form blessing** – Life of the worlds
    B1 Four songs or verse collections – Temple-based, culminating in God's glory and rejoicing
        C **Central psalm: Ashrei**
    B2. Five songs culminating the Book of Psalms - Crescendo of praise
A2 **Subsidiary conclusion** with responsive blessing: "Amen and Amen"
    B3 Chronicles, Nehemiah & Song of the Sea – allusions to both Temples, song of redemption
A3 **Conclusion: Yishtabach with long-form blessing** – Life of the worlds

The overall structure is ABCBA,BA, with the focal point being the twenty-one verses of *Ashrei*.

The following diagram helps us see the relationship of the various "temple-related" sections as well as the obvious parallels of *Baruch She'amar* and *Yishtabach*. The Song of the Sea is thematically related in its final proclamation of kingship, leading into *Yishtabach*.

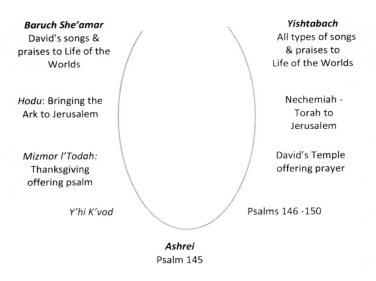

The necklace of Pesukei d'Zimrah:

Baruch She'amar
David's songs &
praises to Life of the
Worlds

Hodu: Bringing the
Ark to Jerusalem

Mizmor l'Todah:
Thanksgiving
offering psalm

Y'hi K'vod

Yishtabach
All types of songs
& praises to
Life of the Worlds

Nechemiah -
Torah to
Jerusalem

David's Temple
offering prayer

Psalms 146 -150

Ashrei
Psalm 145

Chapter 4

From Eternity to Here

After the Verses of Song, if there is a minyan, comes the formal congregational call to prayer: *Barchu et Adonai Ha-m'vorach* – Blessed is *Adonai* who is to be blessed! The congregation responds, *Baruch Adonai HaM'vorach l'olam va'ed* – Blessed is *Adonai*, to be blessed forever.

We enter the third world, *Beriah*, the World of Creation.

In this spiritual environment, on the stage where Scene III is about to begin, the focus is not on tasks and accomplishments, nor the emotional resonances among living beings but, according to the mystics, ideas. This is not ordinary logical thought, deducing and figuring out, solving problems and making conclusions. Those are functions of the brain in service to the World of Action. Rather, in *Beriah* thought is more like contemplation. The word "contemplate" is cognate with "template" and "temple" – it suggests a mode of joining (the prefix "con") with patterns, archetypes, primal thought-forms.

When we consider analogies in our own experience, we might suggest the work of philosophers trying to identify the basic assumptions necessary to the world as we know it, or of scientists seeking the fundamental forces that hold the universe together. In these ways logic and mathematics respond to the yearning we have for understanding the greater whole of which we are a part. But art, music, and other creative endeavors of the imagination also are foundational, though not in the same languages. Jewish liturgy presents foundational elements in a dynamic, poetic way. The prayers in this section display the forces of light, holiness, love, truth, and creativity itself, while inviting us to expand our minds, to imaginatively surround ourselves with the realities those words suggest.

Embedded within this presentation, at its core, is the foundational statement of Judaism: the *Shema*. It is composed of three Torah portions. Sometime in the thousand years before the common era, out of the ancient texts preserved over the centuries, these few paragraphs were chosen to express the Jewish people's commitment to God. One of our treasured mysteries is how this handful of sentences - and primarily six words - became our paradigm. *Shema, Yisrael, Adonai Elohenu, Adonai Echad.* We don't know precisely, but one thing is certain: no company slogan or school motto has ever matched this success story.

The words of the *Shema* represented the essence of the "teaching," which is what the word Torah means, and indeed most of the words come from a dramatic teaching event, the speeches of Moses shortly before his death. Like David in the previous section, Moses - *Moshe Rabbenu*, our teacher - is the character that drives this scene, even though (as in the Haggadah) he is barely mentioned.

The director points us to the first take, in the second millennium B.C.E.

Moses and His People

Following the exodus from Egypt and the revelation at Sinai, the Israelite ancestors of the Jewish people spent a long time in the desert, camping out in various locations for forty years. It was remembered as an arduous and contentious journey. The length of time was itself a product of a problematic event: ten out of twelve appointed spies gave a bad report of the

Land of Israel, frightening their comrades, who then refused to fulfill God's wish that they go forward to conquer the land. In response, God decreed that all the men over twenty years old would die except Joshua and Caleb, the two spies who pleaded with the people to ignore the others' report and undertake the journey. Of all the thousands who had left Egypt, only that generation's descendants would enter the promised land.

At long last, the people approached the borders of the Land, and were ready to cross over. They had already lost two beloved leaders, Aaron and Miriam. They knew that Joshua was the hand-picked successor to Moses, but now they were about to experience the loss of Moses himself. The book of *D'varim* (Deuteronomy) tells us that, in preparation, Moses reviewed the history of their experience together since their time in Egypt, and gave them counsel as to what lay ahead, what challenges they would face, and how to meet them.

Much of Deuteronomy consists of Moses' speeches; interspersed are discussions of laws that will need special attention once they arrive in the Land. The speeches remind the Jewish people -- now mostly the adult children and grandchildren of those who originally left Egypt — of the basic principles, the essential commandments, the overall orientation to life that they will need to sustain. But Moses here is no longer simply the lawgiver, the one who carefully repeats and explains what God has told him. Rather, he is passionate and direct, sometimes warning, sometimes pleading with the people to stay on course.

If we look for that passionate call, *Shema Yisrael!* we quickly see that there are many instances of it. In *D'varim*, we first find it in chapter 5, when Moses says "Hear, O Israel, the statutes and ordinances which I speak in your ears today, that you may learn them...." He continues a few paragraphs later, "Hear therefore, Israel, and be careful to do this, so that it may go well with you and you may increase mightily...." This is followed shortly by the famous line and paragraph that opens our *Shema*.

Still later, Moses will say:

Hear, O Israel, you are to pass over the Jordan today, and dispossess nations greater and mightier than yourself! Hear O Israel, you draw near to battle against your enemies; let not your heart faint; fear not!

"Hear O Israel" is a repeated expression, a rhetorical technique to call attention to the next thing Moses would say. Precisely because it was not unique, we know that it was not only this passionate phrase that persuaded the Sages to choose the passage that would become part of our liturgy. *Shema Yisrael* was a familiar exhortation to carefully listen, attend and observe, so that the people would keep the commandments. Near the end of the book, as Moses is wrapping up his message, he uses it to encourage them to "be of good courage," not to fear the outcome of their venture into the new land.

Something different struck the early creators of this part of the liturgy when they lifted out the paragraph that begins in chapter 6, verse 4. The preceding verse had already said "Hear ...and observe." But now Moses said, "Hear - the Lord our God, the Lord is One - and you shall love Him with all your heart, all your soul, and all your strength." It was the exhortation to love, not the exhortations to obey or be courageous, that the sages first selected.[23] It was the expectation of Moses that "these words will be on your heart" (6.6), to make them part of your relationship with your children, to weave them into your daily life, morning and evening, whether you are sitting at home or on the road (6.7), on your morning commute, or on vacation. Attachment to the one God – a message that certainly was communicated before – Moses now described in personal, everyday terms.

It was also Moses' passionate conviction that this could be done -- that these words would be "in your mouth and in your heart to do it" (Deuteronomy 30.14); he insisted that an intimate relationship with God was possible, and that the commandments could be internalized as part of our lives.

The paragraphs of the *Shema* also included physical reminders - the *mezuzah* scroll at the door, *tefillin* on head and hand, *tzitzit* as an ornament on a four-cornered garment (a standard outer wrap). These would help us remember to bring our commitment into personal and communal reality, encouraging us to integrate all the commandments into daily life.

Moses included as well the promise of the reciprocal action of God: so that "your days will be multiplied, and the days of your children, on the land that the Lord swore to your fathers to give them, as the heavens are over the earth" (Deuteronomy 11.21). We might well wonder at the devotion of our ancestors, repeating this twice daily for two thousand years. They must have had doubts – but they never gave up on the promise of the land we had lost. Today we stand in awe, for beyond all normal hope and expectation, the land has come back to us and we are returning to the land. The promise and the hope had become an indelible part of Jewish life, imprinted each day in our consciousness.[24]

Covenant Renewal

Reciting the *Shema* is a twice-daily reminder of Moses' statement of the essentials of our faith, and the further tangible practices that help us as creatures of flesh and blood. The historian of religions Mircea Eliade has noted that ritual takes us into the formative time of our religious perspective, makes us present in *illo tempore*, "in that time" which conveyed a unique meaning. The mystics suggest that, when we recite the *Shema*, we should imagine ourselves standing at Sinai, or being on the Plains of Moab, hearing the voice of Moses himself ring out. This means not merely remembering that once the Jewish people covenanted with God; we can see ourselves renewing the covenant, personally and as a community.

Covenant renewal ceremonies are described in the Bible. In *D'varim*, Moses specifies one: the reading of the Torah before the whole people every seven years, during Sukkot after the *shmitah* (sabbatical) year. Joshua led a covenant renewal ceremony after bringing the people into the land (Josh. 24). King Solomon renewed the covenant before the people when dedicating the Temple he had built (1 Kings 8). At various times when the people had drifted away from the Torah, usually under the leadership of kings who ignored it, there would be a renewal, as when King Josiah instituted a nationwide reform effort in the sixth century B.C.E. (2 Kings 23). The governor Nehemiah (Nehemiah 9,10) did the same with the Jews who had returned from exile in Babylon.

Rabbinic Judaism added elements of covenant renewal to the pilgrimage holidays of Shavuot and Sukkot, both originally agricultural holidays. Shavuot became the commemoration of "standing at Sinai," and the 8th-day holiday Shemini Atzeret, after Sukkot, became Simchat Torah, "rejoicing of the Torah," when the reading of the Torah began a new cycle.

But reciting the *Shema* was established as a daily renewal. According to the Mishnah, the priests of the Temple recited it in a private daily ceremony apart from the sacrifices. After the Temple's destruction, it became the link for all the Jewish people back to "Moses our teacher" and the transmission of inspiration before he died. One doesn't even have to be praying in a community; every Jew can do this, anywhere in the world or even flying above it.

Yet, humanly, we might well ask: how can we enter this covenant with a whole heart? What does it mean? Moses might try to reassure us, but really, can we do it? Are we even sure we want to? Is it real? We know there is a concept of "accepting the yoke of heaven" (*kabbalat ol malkut shamayim*), and "accepting the yoke of the commandments." But religiously speaking, surely this acceptance is not simply a matter of dutiful performance.

I would suggest a different way of reading this "yoke." In the world of *Beriah*, we are not in ordinary causation, so it is not like yoking an ox to a plow to perform a task, even if the ox is willing to accept. The "yoke" is more like a mountain climber's harness and rope, connecting one climber to another and to the mountain itself. God provides the rope; we receive it (another meaning of *kabbalah*) and tie it on daily for the climb. It is our safety, our surety.

Moreover, the blessings that surround the *Shema* are our guides, preparing our consciousness to make this commitment of renewal. You may recall that we referred earlier to "performative utterances" which create the situation of which they speak. The blessings here lay down the conditions for a key stage of the drama: a transformation of the will, so that we can be partners with God.

Transforming the Will

The first blessing places us fully in the drama of creation, reminding us that the world is a much larger place than we can see with our eyes; it is an entire cosmos, whose source is God. God is identified as Creator (*Yotzer*), and particularly creator and master of light (*Or*).

> Blessed are You, *Adonai* our God, King of the universe, Who forms light and creates darkness, makes peace and creates all.

This reminds the reader immediately of the beginning of the Torah: "Let there be light!" As the power of imagination helped us to see the Temple as symbol of life, to recognize King David's devotion, and to sense the great joy of the people gathered in holiday ceremonies, now we are asked to elevate our minds to imagine creation itself. The various phrases of this long-form blessing show us how to do that by offering anchor points for our minds.

Light and darkness surely allude to the story in Genesis, so that is a starting place. Another aspect is added: "makes peace and creates all." As we will see in many instances from here on, the sages quoted or paraphrased from Tanakh, inviting us to open layers of meaning that connect us more deeply. In this case, the line is an emendation of Isaiah 45.7:

> *[He] forms light and creates darkness, makes peace and creates evil. I am the Lord that does all these.*

Isaiah is making a strong statement of a non-dualistic theology: there is no other deity involved in creation, not even creation of evil.[25] Our text replaces the word "evil" with "all," to avoid the negative, while making the same statement. Stretching beyond the categories of the normal mind, God becomes the source of all.

The blessing continues:

> He illumines the earth and those who dwell on it, with mercy; and in His goodness renews every day, continually, the work of creation.

The word for " illuminates," *me'ir*, is from the same root as "light," but with the force of a dynamic movement – God emanating the light from its source. Now two things are added: God's illumination is merciful and good; and this goodness is connected to God renewing creation "continually" (*tamid*). Continuous creation is a definitive and original theological statement. God didn't create and then go into retirement, like the "clockmaker" God of early modern philosophers, but is engaged in an ongoing process.[26]

Then comes an explicit proof-text for "creates all" from the beautiful Psalm 104.

> *How many are your works, Adonai! Everything in wisdom you have made; full is the earth of your possessions.*

Look at the original Psalm in your Tanakh. You will see a detailed elaboration of the "many works" of God. Biblical scholar Jon Levenson has identified many correlations between this psalm and the creation story in Genesis 1.1-2.3.[27] Our proof-text (v.24) occurs right after the one line in the whole psalm that describes humans:

> *Man goes forth to his action and his labor until the evening. How many are your works, Adonai! Everything in wisdom you have made; full is the earth of your possessions.*

It is humbling to see that this line is all that the psalm has to say about us -- just one of all God's possessions that fill the earth. But that is precisely the point: this humility enables us to transform our will – shifting our willfulness into willing partnership.

To make it possible to covenant with God, we must recognize our true place in a grand and glorious cosmos. In contrast to our smallness, poetic passages emphasize God's strength and glory.

> The King, exalted alone since the beginning of time—
> praised and glorified and elevated from days of old—
> Eternal God,
>> In your great mercies have mercy on us,
>> Lord of our strength, Rock of our refuge,
>> Shield of our salvation, Stronghold for our future.

Similarly, a brief alphabetical acrostic poem provides an interlude (on Shabbat, this is replaced by a longer poem, often sung by the congregation). Translated to capture some of the flavor but not the rhythm and rhyme, it goes roughly as follows:

> א-God, ב-Blessed, ג-Great in ד-Knowledge,
> ה-Prepared ו-And made the ז-Radiance of the ח-Sun!
> ט-Goodness י-Formed כ-Glory ל-For his name!
> מ-Luminaries he נ-Placed ס-Surrounding his ע-Strength!
> פ-Chiefs of his צ-Hosts are ק-Holy ones,
> ר-Exalting the ש-Almighty ת-Always! – telling the glory
>> of God and his holiness.

The alphabetical list is a technique that, among the poets and mystics, alludes to completeness, as we would say "the whole thing, from A to Z." The Light which began the blessing has multiplied into letters and many lights – the sun, stars, and heavenly hosts, led by "holy ones," angels who witness to God's holiness.

The next phrase is an emphatic reply – and may originally have been said by the congregation responsively:

> Be blessed, *Adonai* our God, in heaven above and on earth below, over all the praise of the work of your hands, and over the luminaries of light that you created, glorifying you. Selah!

At this point in the Yotzer Or, with the Selah! we can pause to contemplate the universe from our own cosmological perspective. We know, far more than our ancestors did, of the vast multitude of lights and luminaries, their infinite expanse and their infinitesimal components. We step each day into the immense mystery of an unfathomable universe, infused with vitality and conducted by a divine Intelligence that indeed continually creates anew.

Yotzer Or then shifts into a new key, with a form of the *Kedushah* – a formula for extolling the holiness of God that occurs in several variations in our prayer services. Here, the introduction is clearly intended to inspire us as worshipers:

> Be blessed eternally, our Rock, our King, and our Redeemer, Creator of holy ones – praised be your name forever, our King!—Creator of ministers—and those ministers all stand in the heights of the universe and proclaim — with awe, in one voice, aloud — the words of the God of life and the King of the world.

The "holy ones" of the previous passage are now called "ministers" (*meshartim*) who praise God. A new structure is used here, as we move back and forth from descriptions of these holy beings (A) to the mode of their singing (B) to their shouts of acclamation (C):

A.   [Who are these remarkable beings?]
All are beloved, all are refined, all are mighty, and all do, in dread and awe, the will of their Owner, and
> B.[How do they sing?] All open their mouths in holiness and purity, with song and melody, and bless and praise and glorify and revere and sanctify and crown...
>> C. The Name of God, the great King, powerful and awesome, holy is He!

In a rhythm that, in a kind of quavering, rises higher with each proclamation of holiness and glory, the poem continues:

A.   And all receive on themselves the yoke of heavenly kingship one from another to sanctify their Maker
> B. with contentment of spirit, with pure lips and sacred melody,

A.   All as one,
> B. answering with fear, saying in awe,
>> C. Holy, holy, holy, Adonai of hosts! Full is all the earth of his Glory!

A. And the Ofanim and holy Chayot,
> B. with a great roar,

A. raise themselves toward the Serafim,
> B. facing them, praising and saying,
>> C. Blessed is the glory of Adonai from His place!

The phrases of this Kedushah, in their poetic force as well as their content, portray a model for us as the worshiping congregation. These "pure, refined, holy" singers can suggest an attitude for our approach to praising God. Just as the angels express unity in fear and awe, so can we. Just as they "receive one from another," so can we graciously honor and appreciate our community. Moreover, the mode of the prayer as well as its content conveys new states of being, expressed in emotional and vocal movement, investing the visual concepts of light and glory from the earlier section with the force and vibrancy of sound and voice, surrounding the Holy One.

We will return to these dynamics when we look at the necklace for this blessing, but first let's look at the conclusion. It reprises some themes, but also seems to introduce new ones:

> To God the Blessed they offer sweet melodies; to the King, the living and enduring God, songs they will sing and praises proclaim, for He alone is exalted and holy, performer of mighty acts,
> maker of new things,
> master of wars,
> sower of righteousness,
> causing salvation to sprout,
> creator of healing,
> awesome in praise,
> master of wonders,
> He renews in his goodness every day, continually, the work of creation.
> As it is said, "to the Maker of the great lights, for his kindness is forever."
> Shine a new light on Zion, and may we all soon merit its light.
> Blessed are you, *Adonai*, who forms the luminaries.

Familiar themes include the "living and enduring" God (cf. "life of the worlds" from *Pesukei d'Zimrah*), and the continuous renewal of creation, expressed in words identical to the blessing's beginning. But there seems to be quite a bit of new material – God portrayed as connected to war, righteousness, salvation, healing.

A secret is embedded here. Each of these phrases refers to a power that the ancient world attributed to one of the "seven planets." The sun was the source of might; the moon governed renewal; Mars was the planet of war and bloodshed; "salvation" was associated with the morning and Mercury; Jupiter was guardian of righteousness or justice; Venus brought healing; Saturn, associated with the Sabbath, was a day of "awesome praise."[28]

The text is hinting that whatever powers may be claimed by the planets are actually God's, totally derived from him. When we look into the skies and see the "lights," if we think that they have power and influence over the earth (as in astrology), we should remember that it is God who gives form and meaning to all the luminaries. These phrases, then, are not new statements about God, but an elaboration and revelation of a new dimension of our understanding of the "Creator of Light." As often in chiasmic structures, as we turn back around the oval path, we experience elaboration on, and new insights into, the original theme.

Also parallel to the opening portion of the blessing, another biblical proof-text is brought, this time to elaborate on God's goodness by which he renews creation: "To the Maker of the great lights, for His love endures forever." (Psalms 136:7) Continuous creation includes continuing compassion. If you look at Psalm 136 in Tanakh, you will see that it celebrates both God's creative acts and his conquering Israel's enemies; each verse is followed by *ki l'olam chasdo*, "for His kindness is forever."[29] This also provides a segue into the next *brachah*, which goes beyond *chesed* or kindness, to *ahavah*, love.[30]

A brief additional prayer is added that we all merit to experience "light on Zion," praying that we be allowed to return to our holy land of Israel.

If we outline each of these parts, we can see the chiasmus structure once again. Beginning with creation of Light (singular, or generally), the blessing explores God's greatness over all, His strength like a fortress, and His glory surrounded by lights/hosts. At the center point or pendant is a response, "Be blessed!" Continuing around the other side of the oval, we find holy beings with sounds rather than lights; God's mastery of the planetary powers of healing, salvation; then a text on goodness. In general, God's greatness and light dominate one side, sound and goodness the other. The *chatimah* reflects the *petichah*, but with the emphasis on the multiplicity of lights, the particulars rather than the universal.

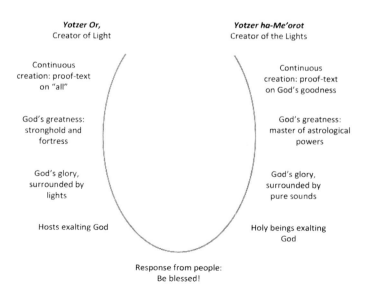

The necklace of Yotzer Or

Yotzer Or,
Creator of Light

Yotzer ha-Me'orot
Creator of the Lights

Continuous
creation: proof-text
on "all"

Continuous
creation: proof-text
on God's goodness

God's greatness:
stronghold and
fortress

God's greatness:
master of astrological
powers

God's glory,
surrounded by
lights

God's glory,
surrounded by
pure sounds

Hosts exalting God

Holy beings exalting
God

Response from people:
Be blessed!

Love and Torah

The second *brachah, Ahavah rabbah,* is simpler than *Yotzer Or.* Thematically, it calls on God our Father and King, who has always shown love and compassion, to continue to teach us as God did with our ancestors. It asks that God instill in the heart of each person a desire to learn and observe the Torah. And finally, it refers to God's power to save, asking Him to bring the people back to their land and close to Him once more.

But this simple summary does not do it justice. This *brachah,* coming right before the *Shema,* is about a particular kind of love, which is deeper and more complex than either modern sentimental or romantic love, and different from the compassion of God's kindness to all creation. We will discuss that further below. But one thing that can help us understand the great significance of this prayer is its emergence at a key moment in Jewish history.

When we look into the history of the *Shema* liturgy (meaning the *Shema* plus the blessings before and after), it turns out we don't know where the *Ahavah rabbah* comes from. We know there was an earlier version of the liturgy, from a passage in the Mishnah that describes a priestly ceremony during the time of the Second Temple.[31] The priests would go, at a certain point in the morning sacrificial service, to a room called the Chamber of Hewn Stones, and the following would occur:

> *The appointed one (of the priests) said to (the others): "Bless one blessing," and they blessed. Then they recited the Ten Commandments, Shema, Vehaya im shamoa, and Vayomer [the three paragraphs of the Shema]. Also they blessed the people with "True and faithful," "Service," and the Priestly Blessing. On Shabbat they added a blessing for the outgoing watch. (M. Tamid 5:1)*

Much of this is familiar to a modern Jew: the Ten Commandments, the three biblical selections, the blessing after the *Shema*, and two other blessings which now appear as the third from last and the last in our *Amidah*. We no longer recite the Ten Commandments, and two blessings are in a different place, but we know the texts – except for the blessing that was said at the beginning. What was that blessing?

Later, people assumed that it was either *Yotzer Or* or *Ahavah rabbah*. Rabbis from the early third century are reported as having different opinions about that:

> *Rabbi Abba and Rabbi Jose came to a certain place, where the people asked them what was the "one blessing" [referred to in the Mishnah], and they could not tell them. They went and asked Rabbi Mattena, and he also did not know. They then went and asked Rav Yehudah, who said to them: "Thus did Shmuel say: It means, Ahavah rabbah. Rabbi Zerika in the name of Rabbi Ammi, who had it from Rabbi Shimon bar Lakish, said: It is Yotzer Or." (B. Berachot 11b)*

In other words, some did not know; and from those who had a tradition about it, there were two different opinions. Some modern scholars agree with the rabbis who said that the blessing said was *Yotzer Or*, because it would have been near sunrise when they were praying during the ceremonies of morning sacrifice, and the blessing for light would be the natural one to say at this time. Moreover, the priestly tradition about creation is alluded to, both directly and indirectly, by reference to Psalm 104. But others disagree. Rabbi Kimelman suggests it wasn't either one, and that most likely they said a blessing over Torah, like one we say now in morning blessings, to precede the saying of *Shema*.

While we still don't know the answer, the fact that the rabbis in the third century were struggling with this question tells us two things: (1) *Ahavah rabbah* and *Yotzer Or* were both well known; and (2) they must have been composed no later than about 150 C.E., because if they had been more recent, one of the rabbis would have had a knowledge of their source. Instead, they remain unattributed.[32]

Ahavah rabbah does, however, have a rabbinic flavor because it clearly emphasizes learning Torah. We know that rabbis began to clearly define the liturgical tradition from the late first century onward. It seems quite possible that one piece of that definition was the composition of *Ahavah rabbah* and its complement in the ma'ariv (evening) service, *Ahavat olam*, sometime in the first half of the second century. The rabbis may have decided that the liturgy should contain a clear statement of God's love for the Jewish people.

Why would that be so? Because the first half of the second century (100-150 C.E.) was a time of increased competition between Rabbinic Judaism and Christianity defined as separate religions,[33] and a key point in their differentiation was a theology of God's love.

For fifty years and more the Christians had been a Jewish messianic sect. But the loss of the Temple in the previous century provoked the question of how to understand this event in terms of God's providence. On the one hand, the Jesus movement thought the loss of the Temple showed God's displeasure, at least with Temple practices. But the event also cast into doubt the early Jewish Christian interpretation of Jesus. He had been presented as the messiah whose resurrection promised the coming kingdom of God, so everyone should repent and be baptized and prepare for the final judgment. After the destruction of the Temple, many thought Jesus would return and announce his kingdom. As the decades wore on and the general resurrection didn't happen, their story was becoming less convincing.

Other versions of the Christian story emerged. Paul, the famous convert from Judaism who became a major Christian evangelist among non-Jews in the years 40-60 (after Jesus had died), had already reinterpreted Judaism to make it easier for non-Jews to join the movement. While he clearly expected Jesus to return as messiah before his (Paul's) generation died off, his letters also were full of spiritual and symbolic interpretations of Jesus' death and its meaning, of baptism as a mystical ritual, and of "faith" on the part of the non-Jew as equivalent to observance on the part of the Jew. His letters to his congregations became very popular and circulated widely after his death.

Accentuating the changes in Christianity, a new story of the life of Jesus appeared around the turn of the second century, between 90 and 110 C.E.. This story or "gospel" purported to be from one of Jesus' original apostles named John (an attribution not supported by scholarship). Communities in Asia Minor - now eastern Turkey and Armenia - were avidly reading this gospel. It portrayed Jesus as the incarnation of the Word (Logos in Greek), thereby replacing the Torah, and it is the most anti-Jewish of the four gospels that are part of the Christian New Testament. Today it is best known for its famous verse which you see on billboards in the countryside: John 3:16. That verse says, "For God so loved the world that he gave his only begotten son, so that whoever believes in him will not perish but have everlasting life." The key message was that the loving God sacrificed his son, Jesus, so that human beings could have salvation. The Johannine gospel helped make

Christianity much less Jewish, speaking of Jesus as the source of eternal life, rather than focusing on a messiah to come soon.[34] Thus, in the early and middle years of the second century, some forms of Christianity were increasingly promoting a message of God's love for the world – and not loving the Jews.

Meanwhile, the Jewish world was in enormous turmoil, for tensions with Rome remained high in the generations after the Temple's destruction. In 132-135, Bar Kochba's army led another revolt against Roman rule and was crushingly defeated. It would not be surprising if Jews were asking, "Does God still love us?"

Through the liturgy, the rabbis of the era could address directly this question and affirm the meaning of God's love for the Jewish people. Perhaps someone from Rabbi Akiva's school composed our *Ahavah rabbah* blessing; for Akiva, who probably lived from about 40 C.E. to 137 C.E., is known for extolling God's love. In *Pirkei Avot*, the saying is attributed to him, "Beloved is Israel, for they were called children of God; and even more beloved, that it was made known to them that they are children of God." Rabbi Akiva also described the Song of Songs as "the holy of holies" (M. Yadaim 3:5), understanding it as a mystical allegory of God's love to Israel.

With that in mind, let us return to the *brachah*. While we do not know the actual composer of the *brachah*, we do know his source: Jeremiah 31.2:

And I have loved you [with] everlasting love [Ahavat olam]; therefore I have drawn you [with] lovingkindness.

This became the basis of the prayer *Ahavat olam*, which in Ashkenazic prayer books has the opening words *Ahavah rabbah*. (Sephardic versions and the ma'ariv prayer for Ashkenazim begin with *Ahavat olam*). This chapter of Jeremiah announces God's promise to restore the Jewish people: "Again I will build you... again will you plant vineyards ... I will turn your mourning into joy. ..."

In our context of studying a blessing that is part of a covenant renewal liturgy, this passage is particularly relevant:

> *I will make with the house of Israel, and the house of Judah a new covenant ; not the covenant that I made with their fathers in the day that I used strength of hand to bring them out of the land of Egypt, a covenant they broke...Rather this is the covenant that I will make with the house of Israel in these latter days, says the Lord, I will give My Torah within them (b'kirbam), and on their hearts will I write it; and I will be their God, and they shall be My people" (Jeremiah 31: 30-32).*

Jeremiah is pointing to the inner dimension of our relationship to God. The prayer composed on the basis of his message stands on that same ground. It definitively turns away from the Christian sacrificial model for God's loving act; and it equally turns away from blaming the people for breaking the past covenant. It focuses on a new covenant, emphasizes a relationship built on inner realities – mercy and compassion on God's part, trust and openness on our part. This is a new prelude to the recital of the *Shema*, where the message of love is redesigned in light of Torah, and Torah in the light of love.

> With abundant love You have loved us, Lord our God,
> With great and extraordinary mercy You have shown mercy upon us.
> Our Father, our King, on account of our fathers who trusted in You,
> and You taught the laws of life,
> Thus be gracious to us and teach us.

What our ancestors did was, most simply, "trust." In contrast with Christian theology, the God who loves doesn't send his son to die, but rather he teaches "laws of life" (*chukei chaim*), through the generations, life to life. In the parallel portion of the *ma'ariv* prayer, *Ahavat olam* speaks of studying the decrees and laws "for they are our life and the length of our days." We aren't asked to "believe in" a theology, but rather to "learn and do" as a process coming from within our hearts, as in Jeremiah's prophecy, "within them." Our prayer pleads,

Instill in our hearts to understand, discern, listen, learn, teach, guard, perform, fulfill what You teach us, in love.

Jews understood God's turning toward humanity not as rescuing them from beyond this world, but as an offer of enlightenment, enlivening, love of the mitzvot, and unification of our hearts to love God in return, in this life. God offers a living and present relationship through the common project of learning.

We can now see, from the historical context, how fundamental the *Ahavah rabbah* was to Jewish life.[35] It was a poem of protest against an unacceptable theology, against a system that was growing in influence and generating negativity against Jews and Judaism. The *Ahavah rabbah* and *Ahavat olam* would stand for us, recited by Jews every day for centuries, asserting God's love for us, and His gift of covenant and Torah, no matter what others might think.

Let's review in more detail, this time with attention to structure, which often highlights significant elements we might not otherwise notice. Thematically this prayer alternates (A) love, including similar terms like compassion and mercy, with (B) teaching and similar terms like enlightening, enabling us to understand. There is also a third part, (C) fulfilling the commandments. Read the prayer and compare with the structure below:

A. With abundant love you have loved us...
   B. to our ancestors, you taught the laws of life.
A. Be gracious to us
   B. and teach us.
A. Have compassion on us
   B. Put it in our hearts, to be able to understand....
      C. and to do and fulfill
   B. all the words of the teachings of Your Torah
A. in love.
   B. Enlighten us in Your Torah,
      C. Make our hearts cling to your commandments,
A. and unify our hearts in love and awe of Your Name, that we may never be ashamed.

The structure – AB,AB,ABCBA,BCA – has an internal chiasmus. But it is a kind of wave structure as well, back and forth from love to teaching, as well as doing.

Clearly, love and teaching/learning are connected. Moreover, the prayer directly addresses the false stereotype of Judaism as being about law rather than love: Law is teaching that relates to living a good life; it is intertwined with love, and indeed is a gift of love.

The model of the loving God is not only parent to child, as in "Ephraim my beloved son" (referred to in Jeremiah 31), nor the model of marriage, which appears most famously in the prophet Hosea, but teacher to student.[36] The love between student and teacher was a powerful experience for our sages. They knew that learning and love happen together because there is a felt relationship, a common heart for the project at hand, something in which both are highly involved and invested. The teacher is giving over what is precious and needed; the student receives it with appreciation and returns the love with wholeness of heart, a heart illuminated with understanding. In this context, the Shema's command "You shall love" means that through understanding – a faculty of the heart in ancient Judaism – you will love from the heart, connected deeply to your vital being.

Love is also connected to a promise for the future, for whatever happens, however the relationship has been disrupted in the past, the covenant still remains, and this passionate love is truly *Ahavat olam*, eternal love. Thus the prayer closes by affirming again our trust that God's salvation will come, specifically in returning us to the land:

> Bring us to peace from the four corners of the earth and lead us upright to our land. For a God that performs salvations are You, and You chose us from every people and tongue, and brought us close to Your great Name, selah, in truth, to offer You thanks and [proclaim] Your Oneness in love. Blessed are You, *Adonai*, who chooses His people Israel in love.

These ending words link directly through the first verse of the *Shema*, which is the proclamation of God's Oneness, to the *V'ahavta*, "You shall love." *Shema Yisrael, Adonai Elohenu, Adonai Echad*, is the connecting link – the gentle kiss, one might say – between the love of God for us, and the love we have for God.

In our prayers, this moment is a good time to pause, before saying *Shema*, to contemplate the extraordinary history of love between God and the Jewish people, sustaining us through millennia. Also we can contemplate and the way that our own experience of divine teaching and guidance has shaped our individual lives. Our personal life, the collective Jewish experience, and the cosmic whole paint a vast canvas where we affirm once again our ability to "hear, O Israel."

Redemption

After the proclamation of Moses, *Shema!* and the covenantal promises -- "You will love... and I will give..." – comes the third blessing of the *Shema* liturgy, which has two parts. The first part, beginning with *emet v'yatziv*, "true and faithful," is part of the renewal of the covenant. We saw this prayer mentioned by the Mishnah as part of the priestly *Shema* recital in the Temple precincts. Imagining the *Shema* as coming from Moses to the community, it is a natural response for the community to say yes, or "True! *Nachon!*" Words are added to elaborate upon the beauty of the covenant and its eternal quality. The response has a strong chanting rhythm:

1) He endures,
2) and His Name endures,
3) and his throne is established,
4) and his kingship and faithfulness forever endure.
5) And his words are living and enduring,
6) faithful and pleasant forever
   i) and to worlds of worlds,
   ii) upon our ancestors and upon us,
   iii) upon our children and upon our descendants,
   iv) and upon all the generations of the seed of Israel
      Your servants,
   v) on the first and
   vi) on the last,
   vii) the Word is good and enduring forever,
7) True and faithful, a decree, and it will not pass away.

In the next section, the theme has switched from the covenant, the "Word," to attributes of God relating to redemption:

True, You are He,
1) Adonai our G*d and G*d of our ancestors,
2) our King, King of our ancestors,
3) our Redeemer, redeemer of our ancestors,
4) our Rock, Rock of our salvation,
5) our Deliverer and Rescuer from forever - Your Name
—and there is no G*d but You.
6) Helper of our ancestors are you from forever,
7) Shield and Savior to their children after them, in every generation to generation.

More affirmations follow. You can see the patterns of sevens, which hint that this is a prayer composed in the priestly style, reinforcing the tradition that it was said in the Temple. There are also six proclamations of "True!" The first three are about enduringness; the last three are about help and salvation. The blessing becomes not simply *Emet v'yatziv*, but also earns its other name of *Ge'ulah*, redemption.

Then the chant shifts to a story, the prototypical Jewish story of redemption, the Exodus from Egypt, now a dramatic narrative told with parallelisms:

From Egypt You redeemed us, Lord our God,
and from the slave-house You delivered us.
All their firstborn You killed,
but Your firstborn You redeemed.
You split the Sea of Reeds and drowned the arrogant.
You brought Your beloved ones across.
The water covered their foes; not one of them was left.

The response from the redeemed people returns to what may by now feel like a familiar poetic form:

> For this, the beloved ones praised and exalted God
> the cherished ones sang psalms, songs and praises
> blessings and thanksgivings to the King, the living and
> enduring God.
> High and exalted
> great and awesome,
> humbling the haughty
> and raising the lowly
> freeing captives
> and redeeming those in need
> helping the poor
> and answering His people when they cry out to Him.

We see paired elements again. Note the similarities to the *Kedushah* portion of *Yotzer Or*:

Yotzer Or: To God the Blessed they [the '**beloved ones**'] offer sweet melodies; to the **King, the living and enduring God, songs they will sing and praises** proclaim...

Ge'ulah: For this, the **beloved** ones praised and exalted God, the cherished ones **sang psalms, songs and praises**, blessings and thanksgivings to **the King, the living and enduring God.**

Also, please recall the "lights" that were attributed to God rather than to planetary powers. We can see structural similarities with the list of actions of God in this blessing:

Yotzer – God's powers   *Ge'ulah*: God's powers
1) performer of mighty acts,   1) humbles the haughty
2) maker of new things,   2) raises the lowly
3) master of wars,   3) freeing captives
4) sower of righteousness,   4) redeeming those in need
5) causing salvation to sprout, 5) helping the poor
6) creator of healing ...   6) answering His people
7) awesome in praise
8) doing wonders

The parallels are striking. We can conclude that the style of this section is coordinated with the *Yotzer Or* before the *Shema*. It even resembles a *Kedushah* - with the "redeemed ones" standing in place of the "holy ones." The redeemed people too proclaim God's holiness, but not only because He is "exalted and alone," but because He is "doing wonders" on earth – which also echoes and amplifies the end of the *Kedushah* of the *Yotzer*.

> Moses and the children of Israel responded with a song of great joy, and they all said, "Who is like You among the mighty, Adonai? Who is like you, majestic in holiness, awesome in praises, doing wonders?" With a new song the redeemed ones praised Your name at the seashore; all as one thanked and acknowledged Your kingship and said, "Adonai will reign forever and ever!"

The blessing concludes, as did the other two *brachot* in this section, with a plea for future redemption:

Rock of Israel, arise to the help of Israel and liberate, according to your word, Judah and Israel. Our Redeemer, *Adonai* of hosts is His name, the Holy One of Israel. Blessed are You, *Adonai*, who redeemed Israel.

Understanding the Shema Liturgy

Before we fully explain this third *brachah*, it is crucial to see it in the context of its structure because, as we will see, this can profoundly affect our experience of its meaning.

The *Shema* section is clearly built on the pattern of chiasmus, ABCBA:

A1. Blessing for creation, *Yotzer Or*
Light, continuous creation; angelic acclamation; litany of God's greatness and goodness
    B1. Blessing for God's love: *Ahavah rabbah*
    Bond with God through love & teaching/learning laws of life
        C. Shema (3 paragraphs)
    B2. Covenantal Pledge: *Emet v'yatziv*, "true and firm"
    Bond with God through loyalty and enduring truth
A2. Blessing for redemption from Egypt, *Ge'ulah,*
Litany of God's goodness; Israelites' acclamation

It is clear that the *Shema* is at the center point of the necklace. On either side are God's love (*Ahavah rabbah*) and our pledge (*Emet v'Yatziv*), in which we return God's love. Bookending those prayers are the story of creation (*Yotzer Or*) and the story of redemption from Egypt (*Ge'ulah*). The parallel intimates that the redemption was like a new creation – the creation of a people parallel to the creation of the universe and its lights. Humans, who were not mentioned in the creation blessing, have come into their own, in a new way.

Now what does the structure mean? If we were to read this in a linear way, it might seem as though creation is the beginning and redemption the end. But as Rabbi Reuven Kimelman points out in his erudite article on the *Shema* liturgy,[37] that's not quite what's going on here. The act of redemption is first generated in the past, as is emphasized by the *chatimah* of *Ge'ulah*, which says "Blessed are You...who redeemed Israel." In contrast, the *chatimot* of the other two blessings use the present tense: "forms the luminaries" and "chooses His people." In *Yotzer Or*, the present is also used in "Who renews every day the works of creation," mentioned twice. Indeed, although we assume creation took place long ago, the *brachah* seems to deliberately avoid placing creation in the past. *Ahavah rabbah* refers to the past in that God taught our ancestors, but also continues "choosing" us, and we trust that God will teach us. These are translated, in the respective acclamations, into "living and enduring" qualities of God: he continually renews, he creates healing, is still master of wars, and continues to help the poor and free captives.

Past and continuing-present converge from all sides, from all three *brachot*. And the necklace structure helps us recognize that the real present moment is in the center between those two stories of past events: the saying of the *Shema*. This is the covenant renewal. The *Ahavah rabbah* asks for this to be deeply imprinted within us through love. In *Emet v'yatziv* we affirm our intent to stay true to this event. All the past actions point to the present – God and us. We stand at the place where the two sides come together. The momentous events of creation and redemption take their meaning from knowing God in the present as our teacher in a loving relationship, ongoing, living and enduring through generations, where we are listening: *Shema Yisrael*.

To put it another way, the chiasmus or necklace corrects our tendency to read these prayers as beginning-to-end and past-to-future. The blessing for redemption is the movement of circling back around the pond, looking at history and at creation from a different perspective, helping us to realize that the aims of creation –continuous creation – and the aims of redemption – generation to generation – are parallel.

What are the aims of redemption? Now we can return to the particular meaning of the third *brachah*, where redemption is alluded to by the description of God's acts.

Humbling the haughty and raising the lowly. Our biblical tradition from the beginning shows an investment by God and by our biblical heroes in overturning what we often call the "powers that be" – certain people who set themselves over others. We can think of how our ancestral traditions challenged the practice of child sacrifice, the status of the firstborn, the *ius prima nocte* (sexual claims of the lord or chieftain), and divine rights of kings. The challenge to power that claims "I made myself!" culminates in the contest between Pharaoh and Moses. But it doesn't end there. Even within our own tradition, prophets confront the power of kings. Power is not allowed to go unquestioned – not even God's power, as shown by Abraham and Moses arguing with God.

Freeing captives and redeeming [or ransoming] the needy. Captives usually refers to prisoners of war, while redemption is usually directed toward those enslaved, with a price on their head. They are "needy" and don't have the money to buy their freedom. But in either case, prison and slavery are two states that, in the ancient world, could be virtual death sentences. Jewish law limited the effects of both these institutions; but in another society, if you crossed the king, you might be thrown into prison not only with no trial but with no limit to your sentence, having hope only that the king might die. Enslavement could easily be for life, unlike under Jewish law.

Helping the poor. Poverty was also considered a terrible fate, not necessarily because of a moral judgment on the poor, but because it was dangerous. Having no money was like having no family – no cushion, as we would say; and no protection. Clearly, too, the poor in ancient times as in ours were more likely to be subject to disease and violence, which could become life-threatening.

All these are very difficult states of being, as we recognize today when we say "it's terrible" to be poor, to be in prison, to be a captive. But bad things can happen, even to good and great people like Abraham and Joseph. Our interpretive tradition often tries to explain and give reasons for such happenings, often in terms of human sin or "measure for measure." The liturgy, however, does not explain. It takes for granted that human beings will have difficulties. What it does claim is that God has the power to reverse these situations, even things that humans imagine are irreversible. To "redeem" is very different than to prevent. Redeeming means, pulling out a person who has fallen into a deep pit, reversing a bottomless slide toward nothingness.[38] It means breaking the chains of hopelessness.

That leads to the last action on the list:

Answering his people when they call out. Just as in Egypt, it was when the people's cry rose to God that the redemption began. God is a listening God, even as we are called to listen in "Hear O Israel." Our sages emphasize over and over again that God wants human speech, expression, prayer.

Often we don't express that need. We see the conditions of life as intractable. "What can you do? It's power politics." "You can't beat city hall." "There's no hope of getting rid of that government." "If you have power and money, you get what you want." "Prison is a dead end." "The poor are always with you." "The universe is deaf to human needs." "Nothing can turn this economy around."

God says "No" to all those human-centered beliefs; and to be in covenant with God, to be in that loving relationship of teacher/student, means we're being trained to listen and to work with God against all those forces that suppress potential, that seem to be dead ends. Part of the work is prayer: we are asking God's help.

Understanding redemption – what it meant in the past, how God continues to manifest it – is essential to being part of the covenant. In other words, it's not that being in the covenant will get you redemption in the future. The situation is reversed: **understanding redemption makes it possible for you to be part of the covenant**. When we have come to the place where we say *Shema*, we understand we are responding to God's glorious creation and God's love. We are making commitments. When we circle around and see the bigger picture, we recognize that at the same time God has been renewing creation day after day, God has also been helping generation after generation. We see the meaning of redemption, where God has invested Godself, and begin to grasp the meaning of the whole enterprise.

These prayers give us the opportunity to transform our will. That is the process of *Beriah*, the World of Creation. Our will is transformed when we align with the deeper purposes of God, rather than living by our own willfulness. Our will is transformed when we give up trying to explain the world, the events of history or the reasons for injustice. And our will is transformed when we recognize that divine creativity and divine love are fundamental – the only things that matter. The world of *Beriah*, we may recall, is considered a world of thought – but not ordinary thought. This world, experienced in the expansiveness of heart-mind knowledge of divine creativity and love, becomes a *tikkun* for our attempts to think and know – a corrective for our philosophies, historical explanations, and all-encompassing theories.

That is why the *Yotzer* offers us glimpses of the grand sweep of creation, from Genesis and the creation of light, to the invisible beings who chant a song of holiness. The blessing reminds us that we are part of something truly much greater than we can imagine or think. If that seems too big for us, the *Ahavah rabbah* comes to tell us we are in a loving relationship with that same Creator, and if we become God's students, we will come to understand. The *Geulah* prayer is the reminder of our historic, and continuing, response.

In this World of Creation, "continually, every day" new things are happening, as we study, reflect, and listen. The rabbis who wrote *Ahavah rabbah* knew this is the "new covenant" that Jeremiah foresaw, "not the covenant I made with your ancestors when I took them out of Egypt." This – the covenant we renew every day when we say the *Shema* – is not about willfully forcing ourselves to do something, like a new year's resolution. It's not about "how much" you "are able to do" or how "strongly" you believe. It is not about strength, power, competition, or lists of achievements. It is about a different kind of will, a willingness rooted in love and connected to all of life, all of creation, in which we play our small but unique part. Commitment means turning our natural potential – each of us individually, and with others who share the vision – to work toward the divine aims for the evolution of creation and humanity. Sharing God's mission, seeking to understand it more deeply each day – that is what it means to "unify our hearts to love Your Name."

When we can seal this new covenant in love and unification with God – affirming True! Beautiful! -- a redemptive vision of the future emerges, on a daily basis. That is the *Ge'ulah* blessing: No longer living in the reality created by Pharaoh, we have made a different choice, and we crossed the sea.

On the other shore is the *Amidah.*

The necklace of the Shema and Its Blessings

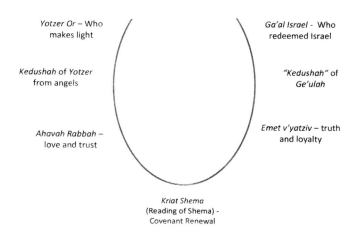

Chapter 5

The Tefillah: Completing the Circle

The last *brachah* after the *Shema* ends on a note of calling to God: "Rock of Israel, rise up to the help of Israel!" So began the redemption from Egypt: The Israelite slaves called out, screamed, shrieked to God, and God heard our cry. At the end of the *Shema* liturgy, we once again call.

But this time, we are in a place of transformation. Rabbi Sacks, in his introduction to the Koren Siddur, notes that the *Amidah* combines elements of both priestly and prophetic prayer. The priestly elements are indicated by the *Kedushah* and the *Birchat Kohanim*, as well as by the public repetition of the *Amidah*; the prophetic aspects are suggested by praying the *Amidah* silently, for prophecy comes from the inner depths.[39] In a sense, we assume the role of priest and prophet, both messengers of godliness, when we say the *Amidah*.

Perhaps that is why the mystics named the Fourth World *Atzilut*, which can mean "nearness" or "nobility," a term appropriate to "a kingdom of priests, a holy nation" (Exodus 19.6). The *Amidah* is an opportunity to present personal requests, as well as prayers for others in need; and yet we do it with a larger consciousness thanks to the spiritual practice in which it is embedded, climbing the "ladder" which brings us through the Worlds.

Still, there is an apparent paradox. If the human will has been transformed and attuned with divine will, what need for prayer? Why not truly silent meditation? Yet words are to be offered; the silence implies privacy, not muteness. The key, I think, is the insistence of Jewish thought that while we may be "near," human and divine are never identical. In that tiny fissure between the greatest mystic or prophet and God is free will, the possibility of difference; and God wants that difference, wants to hear the perspectives, the desires, of His creatures. Judaism's famed examples of prophets questioning God come to mind – a scandal to those who think of faith as submission, or of closeness to God as dissolution of identity. Questions are welcomed, prayers are desired, because the human being is *medaber*, the speaker. Expressing ourselves is a gift to the evolution of the universe.

So our collective prayers are spoken as priests, while hitchhiking on the words of the prophets and psalmists who had learned how to listen and then ask with grace and sincerity.[40] Their words, as we will see, provide the explicit petitions. Our private prayers are like an overtone, barely heard, sometimes spilling openly into speech, sometimes giving a unique color, a whisper of new life, to the prayers.

Let's learn, then, about the vessel that has been created for this silent-speech of calling out to God. As we have seen before, often the structure reveals some of the secrets of the liturgy. So we will begin by looking at the overall structure, then go on to some of the details.[41] You will need to attend to the content of the blessings, so for the next few sections, be sure to have your siddur and your Tanakh within reach.

Secrets of the First Blessing

The *Amidah* has been influenced by the structure of chiasmus – the "necklace," which is familiar to you by now. Three

beginning blessings mirror three ending blessings, with thirteen blessings in the middle.[42] Find these blessings in your siddur, noting where they begin and end:

Blessing 1, *Avot* (ancestors): *Blessed are you Adonai ...* followed by numerous attributes / actions of God...*Blessed are you
Adonai, Shield of Avraham* [in many prayer books: *and rememberer of Sarah* or *and help of Sarah*].

Blessing 2, *Gevurot* (powers) [does not begin with *baruch
ata*, thus signaling a series blessing]: *You are mighty forever, O
Adonai...Blessed are you Adonai, who revives the dead.* (or variation)

Blessing 3, *Kedushah* (holiness): *You are holy and Your
Name is holy...Blessed are You, Adonai, the Holy God.*

Blessing 17, *Avodah* (service): *Be pleased with your people
Israel and their prayers.... and restore the service to...Your house...
Blessed are You, Adonai, who brings back the Shekhina to Zion.*

Blessing 18, *Modim* (thanks): *We thank you, Adonai our
God...Blessed are You, Adonai, The Beneficent [Good] is Your
Name and to You it is fitting to give thanks.*

Blessing 19, *Sim shalom* (peace): *Establish peace, goodness
and blessing...Blessed are You, Adonai, who blesses his people Israel with peace.*

Shield of Avraham our ancestor...reviving the dead...
God's holiness...holy service...thanksgiving...peace. From
this summary of content, it may not be clear how the themes
of the sets of blessings form a chiasmus of the form A-B-C-
C-B-A. Blessings 3 and 17 are a "match," in that #3 speaks of
holiness, and #17 speaks of bringing back the **holy** priestly
service of offerings. But the others are not so clear. To sort

this out, we must first make a detailed excursus into the first blessing, for its unique character is often overlooked.

The first blessing clearly includes descriptions of God – attributes such as great, awesome, beneficent, etc. But because we don't know our biblical literature very well, modern Jews do not realize that many of these attributes come directly from events in the history of the Jewish people.

We tend to miss, for example, the fact that while the blessing starts with *Baruch ata Adonai Elohenu*, it does not continue with the usual formula of calling God the king, *melech ha-olam*. Rather, it says "God of our fathers, God of Avraham, God of Yitzchak, God of Yaakov."[43] The threefold reference to the God of the patriarchs is unique and notable for its first occurrence – namely, at the Burning Bush, God's first direct revelation to Moses. God announces that he has come to save the Israelites, and soon will reveal a new name by which the patriarchs did not know God.

And He said: Do not come near. Take your shoes off your feet, for the place you are standing on is holy ground. And He said: I am the God of your father, the God of Avraham, the God of Yitzchak, the God of Yaakov. (Exodus 3.5-6)

The three-patriarchs reference is repeated several times in the narrative in chapters 3 and 4 of the book of Exodus. To use this phrase in the *Amidah* is to say, in effect, "God from the burning bush." It points to God as the Holy One who promises to redeem the people, by sending Moses to Pharaoh and demanding the release of the Israelites.

The sages are addressing God with an expression, or "name," used in the Torah. That gives us a clue. If we pursue this line of thinking, we will see that the next phrase, *ha-gadol ha-gibor v'ha-norah* ("great, mighty, and awesome") also has a unique place. Moses used it when he spoke to the people on the plains of Moab before his death, reminding them of God's compassion to the unfortunate and the great redemption from Egypt that God had performed, and urging them to act justly and kindly as well:

> *The Lord your God is God of gods, and Lord of lords, the great, mighty and awesome God, who does not regard persons or take a reward. (Deuteronomy 10.17)*

This is God the true judge, as seen through the eyes of Moses. The same phrase is used again nearly a millennium later in Nehemiah 9:32, when the governor of the returned exiles describes the history of God redeeming the people:

> *Our God, great, mighty and awesome God, keeper of the covenant and the kindness, let it not be a small thing before You, all the travail that came upon us, ... from the days of the kings of Assyria to this day...*

This name speaks of God acting in integrity, justice and kindness, keeping His covenant.

The next phrase in the blessing addresses God as El Elyon, God Most High, a very ancient divine name that rarely occurs in this combination in the Bible. We find it in the Torah in an episode involving Avraham, which we mentioned in the first chapter. Avraham, then named Avram, has just helped to defeat four oppressive kings and freed his nephew Lot from captivity. He is greeted by a priest-king named Melchizedek:

And Melchizedek king of Salem brought forth bread and wine; and he was a priest of El Elyon (God Most High); and he blessed him, and said: "Blessed be Abram of El Elyon, Maker of heaven and earth, and blessed be El Elyon, who has delivered your enemies into your hand." (Genesis 14:18-20)

The clear implication is that Avraham succeeded because he was "blessed of God the Most High." God here is the one who helps against all odds, and "delivers your enemies into your hand," ensuring victory in a just war.

Gomel hasadim tovim, "bestower of good kindnesses" is an expression for God derived from a verse in Isaiah, when God speaking through the prophet reminds us of the good He has done, in times when divine anger was visited upon many other peoples:

...the great goodness toward the house of Israel, which He hath bestowed on them according to His mercies, and His many kindnesses. (Isaiah 63.7)

This became a well-known phrase from a blessing the Talmud, "Blessed is God who bestows lovingkindnesses," which according to Rabbi Yehudah should be said after one of the four deliverances from major trouble (Berachot 54b). We use a somewhat different version today (see Koren Siddur, pp 162-63). A similar phraseology occurs in the *Bircat hamazon* (grace after meals), where God is described as the one who "bestowed, bestows, and will bestow grace, kindness, and mercy forever."[44] The contexts in all these instances yield the idea that terrible things can be happening, or one can be in a horrific situation, but God never stops saving people and doing good, though it may be harder to see.

God is next described as *Koneh ha-kol*, often translated "creator," but more literally "owner of all," which does not occur in exactly that form in Tanakh, but the idea is present in a few places. In the same chapter in *D'varim* as "great, mighty, and awesome," we read:

> *Behold, to the Lord your God belong the heavens, the heavens above the heavens, [and] the earth with all that it is in it. (Deuteronomy 10.14)*

In the same verse as the name *El Elyon*, God is described as "owner of heaven and earth"; and Psalm 24.1 gives us the familiar verse, "The earth is the Lord's, and the fullness thereof."

The next phrases also do not have exact equivalents in Torah, but we can find allusions in *Nevi'im* (Prophets):

Zocher hasdei avot, "who remembers the kindnesses of your ancestors," most likely refers to a tender passage in which God speaks fondly of the loyalty of the Jewish people, particularly when they left behind the civilization of Egypt for the desert and beyond:

> *I remember the kindness of your youth, the love of your bonding; when you followed me into the wilderness, in a land that was not sown. (Jeremiah 2.2)*

U'mevi goel.... "And brings a redeemer to their children's children ..." This speaks of God's promise of a redeemer, in an indefinite future time, to our "children's children." It alludes to a promise in Ezekiel (*Yechezkel*):

> *And they shall dwell in the land that I have given unto Jacob My servant, wherein your fathers dwelt; and they*

shall dwell therein, they, and their children, and their chil-
dren's children, forever; and David My servant shall be
their prince forever. (Ezekiel 37.25)

Ezekiel goes on in this passage to speak of God's promise of
an everlasting covenant and a temple that will last eternally.
When our prayer says, "for the sake of His name in love," it
probably refers obliquely to the same passage, where God's
reputation (i.e., His good "name") among the nations is
mentioned:

I will be their God, and they will be my people; and the
nations shall know that I am the Lord that sanctify Israel.
(Ezekiel 37: 27-28)

"I will be their God, and they will be my people," also expresses the covenantal love between us.

All these allusions are highly encoded in the brief phrase,
"and brings a redeemer.... in love." Why encoded rather than
quoted directly? Possibly the sages were being cautious about
direct allusions to prophecies of redemption. After the disas-
trous defeats of the Jewish armies in 70 C.E. and again in 135
C.E., knowing that the Roman rulers were alert to charges of
sedition, the verses of ancient prophecy may have been toned
down or referred to by allusion.

Melech, ozer u'moshiah u'magen. "King, Helper, Savior, and
Shield" leads up to the *chatimah.* Perhaps surprisingly to many
of us, God is rarely referred to in Tanakh as king, but proba-
ble references for other parts of this list are the following, in
Psalms – so that at the end of the *brachah,* we have moved
from the historical review to acclamations of praise:

To rescue their soul from death, and to sustain them in famine. Our soul longed for the Lord; Our help and our shield is He. (Psalms 33.19)

Israel, trust in the Lord! Their help and their shield is He! House of Aaron, trust in the Lord! Their help and their shield is He! You that fear the Lord, trust in the Lord! Their help and their shield is He. (Psalms 115:9-11)

The Lord is my rock, my fortress, and my rescuer; my God, my rock; in him I take refuge; my shield, the horn of my salvation, my high tower. (Psalms 18.3)

The specific *chatimah*, "shield of Abraham," comes from the aftermath of the war of the kings in Genesis 15, when God says to Abraham, "Fear not, I am your shield."

This lengthy examination of just the first *brachah* of the *Amidah* helps us see two things. First, the Sages who composed the *Amidah* repeatedly turned to Tanakh to express their understanding of God's work, the divine manifesting itself in the world. As Rabbi Elie Kaunfer puts the issue: "Prayer is not only about us trying to throw adjectives at God, but about listening to the ways in which God is speaking to us. What is the message of God's speech?"

Second, this *brachah* focuses on many specific references to God's saving acts: assisting and protecting Abraham, redemption from Egypt, providing for the people in the wilderness, judging their enemies, bringing the people back to the land, and a future redemption, yet to be revealed. The only phrase that does not refer to a redemptive act of some kind is *koneh hakol*, "owner of all." God as creator plays a small part here; God as redeemer a large one.

This *brachah* takes up where *go'el Yisrael* left off at the end
of the *Shema* liturgy: Redemption is everywhere (not only
at the Red Sea), ongoing through history, and promised for
the future. Moreover, in the chiasmic structure of the *brachah*, the epithet "owner of all" fits beautifully. Look carefully at the content here:

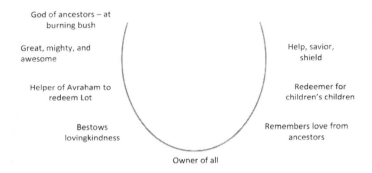

God's greatness parallels God's goodness – a pattern we
have seen before. Abraham being helped by God to redeem
Lot parallels the prayer for a redeemer. God's bestowal of *hasadim* – acts of love – has a reflection in the *hasdei avot*, the
love that drew them after God in the wilderness. The pendant
is marked by the unique and universal name "Owner of all,"
while the opening name is very particular, God of each of the
patriarchs.

This enables us to see the hidden richness of the first
blessing. Many commentators have said that the purpose of
the first three blessings is to offer praise and thanksgiving,
because we should appreciate and thank someone – especially a king – before asking him for something. While true,

the same could be said of most prayer in the ancient world. We can now clearly see in the first blessing that the mode of address is not merely a protocol of politeness, and much less is it random terms of praise; these are names for God as redeemer in quite specific ways. We, as the praying community, are invited through these names to re-imagine these historical and existential situations, in which we participate as heirs of Jewish tradition. The names are not a formal address, but on the contrary an invitation to intimacy, to know this God who is helper, rescuer, and protector.

Perhaps unfortunately, this puts in question the modern egalitarian additions to this *brachah*. The reference to the God of Abraham, Isaac and Yaakov at the beginning has nothing to do with favoring men over women, nor even with the lives of the patriarchs. This name of God reminds the community and the individual of an epiphany, a transformative event in the life of Moses and then the Jewish people – the Burning Bush.

If we want to add appropriate attributes to this list that include women, we should examine how God's redemption was activated through women. In that light, the Conservative rendering of the *chatimah*, "shield of Abraham and rememberer of Sarah" (*fo-ked* Sarah), may be preferable to the more general term "helper" of Sarah as found in the Reform version. But we would be wise to understand that, in quoting God speaking to humans, the rabbis were trying to convey a different message. That said, it might be an enhancement to this *brachah*, and an honoring of its deeply biblical spirit, to find names of God that reflect God's redemptive relationships with the women of Tanakh.

Beginning and Ending Blessings

Understanding that the first *brachah* is about specific acts of redemption throughout Jewish history, we can now return to the structure. The second blessing, which is about the life-giving and life-restoring powers of God, seems much simpler. It announces God's power over rain and wind, the changes of seasons, as well as the ability to heal, free captives, and support "the fallen." We celebrate in this blessing the miracles of nature — how rain returns to the desert, how plants emerge from the frozen earth. We remind ourselves that God has power over the circumstances that cause pain and dislocation.

Even more, this blessing asserts the ultimate power — over death. This message is difficult for moderns. In the view of the rabbinic authors of this blessing, the greatest exemplification of the life-giving aspect of God's nature is resurrecting the dead, *mechayeh ha-metim*. Most striking is the fourfold repetition, in the traditional version of the prayer, of God's power over death, in addition to an allusion to being "faithful to those who sleep in the dust" (cf. Daniel 12:2). Where humans fear ultimate defeat by nature, this blessing affirms the opposite: ultimate victory.

Historically, the idea of the resurrection of the dead – the literal return to life of those who had died – was hotly debated in the early centuries of the common era, and possibly for generations before. The Pharisees, who were the intellectual ancestors of our rabbinic tradition, held to a belief in resurrection. The Sadducees, who tended to be of the aristocratic and/or priestly families and involved with the government, denied and denounced that belief, apparently because it was not written in the Torah. The Christians, who emerged in the middle of the first century C.E. as a new Jewish sect, claimed not only the Pharisees' belief but also that their teacher had in fact been resurrected from the dead.

The rabbis' strong insistence on *techiat hametim* is surprising to many Jews today. But Jewish belief in resurrection was in many ways a natural extension of a theology that celebrated life and creation. If God could heal the sick, free captives, and restore strength to the weak, it was only one step more to revive the dead.[45] Indeed, if death stood in the way of God, then one could not really claim God's omnipotence. Resurrection also was not an individual matter, but was linked to the restoration of the entire Jewish nation in its own land. After two devastating wars with Rome, such restoration might have seemed almost as unlikely as resurrection, but it was also in line with promises that had come through the great prophets.

Prophetic vision links this blessing with the previous one, for the chapter alluded to with the phrase "You will bring a redeemer," Ezekiel 37, is the chapter containing Ezekiel's vision of the "dry bones," a parable for the ultimate restoration. We tend to simplify these matters as natural cycles of rain and dew, or sleeping and waking; but those were not merely "natural" in the ancient world. (Even today, we may understand rain, but we can't fix drought by "making it rain.") For our sages, the promise of redemption was more than implied: it was the ultimate affirmation of the God of life, the "living and enduring God" of *Emet v'yatziv*, and the "life of the worlds" of *Baruch she'amar* and *Yishtabach*.

As we noted, the third *brachah* is the proclamation of God's holiness. When there is a minyan, the *Kedushah* is recited in full, the earthly congregation reciting the words of the angels. Again we receive these words from the prophets Isaiah and Jeremiah, and add an affirmation from Psalms.

Isaiah's vision came to him in the Temple, where he saw God on His throne, and seraphim standing above him:

And they call to one another saying, "Holy, holy, holy is *Adonai* of hosts; the whole world is filled with His glory."

Ezekiel in his chariot vision heard the angels saying,

Blessed is the glory of *Adonai* from His place.

The congregation acclaims with a verse from Psalms 146,

Adonai shall reign forever. He is your God, Zion, from generation to generation. Halleluyah!

Clearly this is the epitome of descriptions of God – Holy! Holy! Holy! Yet there is mystery here too. In the longer version of the *Kedushah* at *Musaf* (the additional service for Shabbat and holy days), the angels ask, "Where is the place of His glory?" The *Kedushah* points to a dimension of God which even the angels cannot fully understand. The response, in that *Kedushah*, is the *Shema*: "Hear, Israel – *Adonai* is our God." We stand in the presence of mystery, not understanding; and at the same time we are reassured that this is indeed God's presence; we are God's and God is ours.

Now we can summarize how the first three *brachot* fall into place.

Blessing #1: God directly acting in Jewish history, saving people individually and collectively;
Blessing #2: God's commitment to all life, specifically in giving life and conquering death;
Blessing #3: God's presence with us from an unknowable dimension called "holiness."

Let's compare those with the ending blessings. We noted that the seventeenth, called *Avodah*, asks for acceptance of our prayers, then requests restoration of priestly service and acceptance of Israel's "fire offerings" and prayers. "Restoring the *Shekhina* (Divine Presence) to Zion" also means making Zion - or Mount Zion, the place of the Temple – holy once again. Thus blessing seventeen corresponds with the holiness acclamation of blessing three.

The eighteenth blessing, *Modim*, has two versions. One, which is said by all in private prayer and by the *chazzan* in repetition, thanks God using the terms Rock and "Shield of our salvation" for God, and also "for our lives which are entrusted to Your hand, for our souls placed in Your charge," for miracles, wonders, and favors "at all times." Insertions for Hanukkah and Purim are placed in this *brachah*, emphasizing thankfulness for direct support, even intervention, by God.

The other version is said silently by the congregation while the chazzan says the first. In the early centuries of our liturgy, it was a brief response by the congregation to the leader's Modim, which was the last prayer before the priests took over to say the priestly blessing. But there were several versions of the response, from different rabbinic traditions ranging from the third to mid-fourth century. In the late fourth century, Rav Papa decided that an amalgam of the responses would be the best choice (B.Sotah 40a). That became our prayer, now called Modim de Rabbanan (Modim of the Rabbis) because it was from several rabbis.

These responses particularly emphasized the blessings of God's creation, life, and sustenance. (In addition, one of the responses asked for return of the exiles.) The words of the prayer now remind us of the familiar blessing of "Shehechianu," said at times of eating new fruit or wearing new clothing, fundamentals of life.

> God of all flesh, the one who formed us and formed the universe: Blessings and thanks to Your great and holy Name for giving us life and sustaining us; may you continue to give us life and sustain us.

While the two Modims are complementary, the first places emphasis on the ancestors and the wonders and miracles of our history (including Hanukkah and Purim), while the Rabbis' Modim places more emphasis on the sustenance of daily life. These happen to correspond with the two different themes of the first two *brachot* of the Amidah. We can label the first as 18A, thanks for God's acts of redemption, and the second as 18B, thanks for God's power in sustaining life.

The 19th blessing prays for peace kindness, grace, and mercy, and God's gift of the "light of Your face" to all the people. It follows on the priestly blessing for peace, and concludes the whole structure.

This gives clarity to the chiasmic structure of the first and last three blessings of the Amidah, with blessing #18 paralleling both #1 and #2:

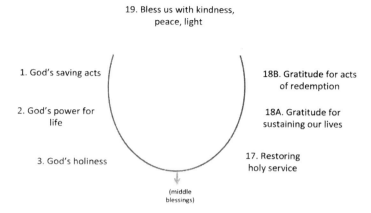

These blessings, opening and closing this fundamental prayer, show us how to "stand" firmly in a knowledge of God and a meaningful relationship with God. We may remember that at the giving of the Torah, the people fainted in the presence of God; they could not stand. The *Amidah*, "Standing prayer," asks us to speak, and reminds us before whom we stand. The first blessing says: our people have a long and deep history with God. The second blessing tells us that our very life force depends on God. The third reminds us that even those great things are only the finite aspects of the God we call "holy." The ending blessings ask God to receive our prayers as if they were fire-offerings from our hearts; and thank God for sustaining our lives on a daily basis and continuing to act in our history to keep us alive. From this place, whether the middle blessings are those of Shabbat or a holiday, or the ordinary weekday, we can learn to trust: we are communicating with a God who is engaged in the world, who overcomes the forces of decay and death, and who extends beyond even life and death into realms we cannot imagine.

The Middle Blessings

The thirteen middle petitions are embedded in a series, which means the "*Baruch ata....* " formula, is not repeated in each blessing. Unlike the Morning Blessings, these are in the plural (us, with Hebrew ending –*nu*), not the singular. Most importantly, as we noted earlier, the blessings of the *Shemoneh esreh* take their cue from specific words of the prophets and psalms – God's promises, the testimonies of those who truly knew God and, as Abraham Joshua Heschel said, experienced the divine pathos or feeling-consciousness.[46] In reciting the prayers, we are often speaking God's words back to Godself, listening and learning to discern the divine intent. We'll examine the content of the blessings, and then come back to what it means to hear and then speak the language of prophets. Through this we will come to understand more deeply something of what it might mean to be in the World of Nearness, *Atzilut*.

The thirteen blessings in the middle also form a structure, but it has some variations, as this was the most flexible part of the service, and changes have been made in the versions that have come down to us.[47] Much ink has been spilled over how the blessings fit together and can be understood historically, but I have chosen an interpretation from Rabbi Elie Munk, which is very useful for remembering the relationships among the blessings.[48]

According to Munk, the first three blessings of the middle thirteen have to do with the spiritual well-being of the individual. In other words, these are inner dimensions of individual well-being. First we ask for knowledge and understanding; second, that God bring us back to our true selves in *teshuvah*, and third, that we be forgiven for our errors and sins. A verse from Isaiah states that if the people "with their heart will understand,

they will return and be healed"(6.10).[49] That is the process the
Amidah mediates in these three blessings (#4, #5, #6).

> 4. You grace the human being with knowledge, and
> teach men understanding. Grace us from Yourself
> with knowledge, understanding, and discernment.
> Blessed are You *Adonai*, gracious Giver of knowledge.
>
> 5. Bring us back, our Father, to your Torah, and bring
> us close, our King, to Your service, and influence us
> to return in complete repentance (*teshuvah*) before
> you. Blessed are You *Adonai*, who desires repentance.
>
> 6. Forgive us, our Father, for we have erred; pardon us,
> our King, for we have sinned; Pardoner and Forgiver are
> you. Blessed are You, *Adonai*, Gracious one abundant in
> forgiveness (or, Who forgives abundantly).

However, these blessings do not convey the urgency of their
sources. In the Isaiah text, the prophet understood from God,
who declared that the people had become spiritually obtuse, that
their situation was desperate. Similarly, the fifth *brachah* alludes
to a verse from the end of *Eicha*, Lamentations, traditionally attributed to Jeremiah. The entire text is one of mourning over the
destruction of Jerusalem in the sixth century B.C.E. It does end
on a note of hope in God: "Bring us back to you, Lord, and we
shall return; renew our days as of old." (Eichah 5:21)

Further, the sixth *brachah* contains language similar to
Yom Kippur prayers. Naming God as *Avinu* and *Malkenu*, it
uses the words *selach* and *mochel*, often translated "forgive"
and "pardon," and verbs from *chet* and *pesha*, "error" and "sin."
From the statement in Psalm 86, "For you, Lord, are good
and forgiving and abundantly kind to all who call upon you,"
(86.5), the sages created the *chatimah*.

Understanding their context, we can recognize that the prayers for knowledge, *teshuvah*, and forgiveness are very serious. We call ourselves to account and ask for reconciliation, a healing of spirit.

The next group of blessings has to do with material blessings on the individual, that is, the external dimensions of personal life: #7 with the removal of conflict, #8 with healing from illness or injury, and #9 with sustenance or livelihood:

> 7. See our affliction and champion our cause and redeem us speedily for the sake of your name, for a strong Redeemer are You. Blessed are You *Adonai*, Redeemer of Israel.

Redemption here seems to refer to social conflict, because *riva rivenu* (here translated 'champion our cause') often refers to quarrels or court cases. God is being asked to be our advocate in difficult situations. This reminds us again that, for the sages, redemption could refer to rescue or relief from a wide range of conditions. The proof-text is from Psalms, in a section which praises God's laws and asks for protection from those who do not respect the laws:

> *See my affliction and release me, for Your Torah I have not forgotten. Champion my cause (rivah rivi) and redeem me; for Your Word, preserve me. (Psalms 119: 153-54)*

You can see there how the singular was changed to the plural, in a close adaptation of the biblical verse, just as in #5. Similarly in the following:

> 8. Heal us, *Adonai*, and we will be healed; save us, and we will be saved; for You are our praise. And bring complete healing for all our wounds, for You, God, King, are a faithful and compassionate healer. Blessed are You, *Adonai*, Healer of the sick of His people Israel.

Jeremiah's prayer, which provides the source, came at a time of great distress, when he saw that his only hope was to hold onto God:

Heal me, Adonai, and I will be healed; save me and I will be saved, for You are my praise. (Jeremiah 17.14).

The end of this group of three is the prayer for sustenance, which has one phrase that changes in the winter season, adding a request for dew and rain.

9. Bless upon us, *Adonai* our God, this year and all the varieties of crops, for good; and grant [dew and rain as] a blessing on the face of the earth, and satisfy us from Your goodness, and bless our year like the best years. Blessed are You *Adonai*, Blesser of the years.

Unlike the others thus far, this *brachah* does not have a near-equivalent in Tanakh. Our sources mention Hosea 6: 1-3 which, although it isn't a direct source for our blessing, beautifully connects spiritual and material: "And may we know, eagerly strive to know the Lord; His going forth is sure as the morning; and He shall come unto us like the rain, as the late rain that waters the earth."

These six blessings (#4 through #9) are perhaps best summed up in this verse:

Bless the Lord, my soul, and forget not all His kindnesses -- the One who forgives all your sins, heals all your diseases, redeems your life from the pit, and crowns you (with) kindness and mercy. (Psalms 103.2-4)

Next follows a blessing, #10, that bridges the individual concerns of the previous six with the collective or communal concerns of the following blessings – namely, a prayer for bringing the entire Jewish people together again.

> 10. Blow the great shofar for our freedom, and raise the banner to gather our exiles and gather us together from the four corners of the earth. Blessed are You, *Adonai*, Gatherer of the dispersed of His people Israel.

Again there are biblical sources. The shofar-blowing comes from a legal text about the jubilee year, when the shofar was sounded to announce that slaves were freed and debts were forgiven:

> *Make a proclamation with the blast of the shofar on the tenth day of the seventh month, on the day of atonement you will be making a proclamation with the shofar through your whole land. And you will sanctify the fiftieth year, proclaiming liberty throughout the land to all its inhabitants.* (Leviticus 25.8-10)

The gathering of exiles comes from a prophecy in Isaiah, in the same chapter as the famous "the wolf shall dwell with the lamb and the leopard lie down with the kid":

> *And He will raise up a banner for the nations, and assemble the castaways of Israel, and the scattered of Judah He will gather from the four corners of the earth.* (Isaiah 11.12; compare 27:13)

That tenth blessing is the center of the "necklace" – nine blessings before and nine after.

Several blessings for communal well-being follow. Recall that the order of the previous six individual spiritual blessings was knowledge, *teshuvah*, and forgiveness. Communal spiritual blessings have to do with ethics and morality. But Judaism recognizes that in a community, wisdom and ethics are expressed through people, not merely ideas – a point often forgotten when we attach ourselves to "isms." Thus we begin with a request for people who can administer justice with wisdom, "as in the beginning." (One of Moses' first acts after coming out of Egypt, recounted in chapter 18 of Exodus, was the establishment for the people of a hierarchy of judges, on the advice of his father-in-law Jethro.)

> 11. Restore our judges as at the first and our counselors as in the beginning. Remove from us sorrow and groaning, and reign over us – You, Lord, alone – with kindness and compassion, and rectify us with justice. Blessed are You, Lord, King who loves righteousness and justice.

Isaiah's first prophecy is the foundation for that prayer. God's judgment is that "the faithful city has become a harlot," but God will cleanse the people of their sins and bring the city back to its foundations of justice:

Then I will return Your judges as at first and your counselors as at the beginning, after that you shall be called City of Righteousness, Faithful City.
(Isaiah 1.26)

The next two blessings, #12 and #13, address the ultimate moral problem: the eradication of evil and the strengthening of good in the Jewish people's collective inner life. Again, evil and good are not abstract but are embodied in people. In these prayers

God is called on to take action against the wicked to remove their power, while both compassion and reward are requested for those who trust God and represent the highest ideals. The wicked:

> 12. For slanderers may there be no hope; and may all evil in an instant perish; and all Your enemies speedily be cut down; and brazen sinners may You speedily up-root, shatter, cast down, and humble, speedily in our days. Blessed are You *Adonai*, Shatterer of enemies and Humbler of the brazen.

Minim, here translated slanderers, can mean heretics or apostates, or possibly informers.[50] Note that it referred to enemies internal to the community, that is, Jews whose actions and words threatened the safety or the whole people or integrity of our collective mission (whereas threats from external enemies required prayers for salvation or redemption).

The metaphors of "cutting off" and "uprooting" come from a late prophetic book, that of Malachi:

> *For behold the day will come, burning like an oven, and it will be that all the brazen and all that do evil shall be stubble, and that day will set them ablaze, says the Lord of Hosts, that will leave them no root or branch.* (Malachi 3.19)

Malachi was written after the return from Babylonian exile in the period of the Second Temple. In that book, the Jewish people are questioning God's love for them – a situation which, as we noted earlier, may have been occurring in the era of the composition of the *Amidah*. If people from within our own ranks were raising that question, the spiritual danger was indeed extraordinary. No wonder that Rabban Gamliel felt it urgent that someone compose a prayer regarding the minim (see Berakhot 28b), and Malachi was the inspiration.

To preserve and nurture goodness, the next blessing asks:

> **13. Upon the righteous and on the devout, on the elders of Your people the Family of Israel and on the remnant of their scholars, on the righteous converts and on ourselves, may Your compassion be aroused, *Adonai* our God, and give good reward to all who trust in Your name in truth. Establish our portion with them forever, that we not be ashamed, for in You we trust. Blessed are You *Adonai*, Steadfast and Trusted One for the righteous.**

For the sages, the issue was clear: trust in God, and keep close to the community that is in alignment with God's law. Be like Isaiah, who speaks of his personal experience in holding to God despite those who ridiculed him:

> *Who among you fears the Lord, listens to the voice of His servant? Though he walks in darkness, and has no light, let him trust in the name of the Lord, and be steadfast in his God. (Isaiah 50.10)*

The reference to listening to "the voice of His servant," namely the respected prophet, would mean something different in rabbinic times – relying on and listening to the elders, scholars, and others who stood up for good in the community and so were referred to as "the righteous."

Interestingly, the next set of blessings, having to do with the material welfare of the community in Munk's understanding, do not refer to what consumes the thoughts of modern Westerners – a country's economic system. Rather, blessings #14 and #15, allude to external, long-lasting communal structures that generate national health: the restoration and stability of the holy city, and of the dynasty of David:

> 14. And to Jerusalem, Your city, in compassion may you return and dwell in her midst, as You have spoken. And rebuild her soon in our days, an everlasting edifice, and the throne of David speedily establish in it. Blessed are You, *Adonai*, Builder of Jerusalem.

> 15. The sprout of David Your servant may you speedily cause to sprout up, and exalt his horn in Your salvation, because for Your salvation we hope every day. Blessed are You, *Adonai*, Who makes flourish the horn of salvation.

The first of these two comes from Zechariah, after a plea from the prophet to God:

> *Therefore, thus says the Lord, I will return to Jerusalem in compassion, My house shall be built in it, says the Lord of Hosts...Sing and rejoice, daughter of Zion; for, behold, I come, and I will dwell in your midst, says the Lord. (Zechariah 1.16, 2.14)*

The second is from Jeremiah, in a chapter promising restoration – with the famous verses we sing at weddings, "Again it shall be heard in this place, *kol sasson v'kol simcha, kol chatan v'kol kallah* -- the voice of joy and the voice of gladness, the voice of the bridegroom and the voice of the bride" (Jeremiah 33.11). It goes on to prophesy the righteous leader:

> *In those days at that time I will cause a sprout of righteousness to sprout forth for David, and he will administer justice and righteousness in the land. (Jeremiah 33.15).*

In Psalm 18, David specifically calls God "my horn of salvation". "Sprouting" a "horn of salvation" is a way of saying that God will carry out His ultimate purpose through the dynasty of David. It suggests the vigor of a young animal, sprouting horns as it comes to maturity -- not instantaneous, but growing over time.[51]

These blessings, particularly the ones concerning a Davidic messiah, are sometimes difficult for modern Jews. The lineage of David is hard to understand in any literal sense. It could be interpreted to mean simply a belief in a messiah (whether his lineage is known or not), but even that is difficult to assimilate, and has been removed from many non-traditional prayer books. Nevertheless, we are apparently not the first to raise concerns about these political structures, because the blessings are not completely consistent with one another.

Both blessing 14 and 15 mention the Davidic expectation – one referring to the throne of David, the other to the sprout. Blessing 14 begins with the conjunctive *vav* ("And…"), suggesting that it has been separated from another blessing. Even blessing 11, which asks "Reign over us – You alone, O Lord" and calls God "King" may reflect the ancient Jewish tension over human versus divine kingship (although one could take this less literally and argue that the blessing only refers to judges who implement God's laws). In any case, we can assume these formulations were sometimes contested, as communities discussed and debated how to pray about these matters.

The overall intent of the communal blessings is clear, however: we need honest, devoted, and skilled leadership that can unify our people, and we love and honor the ancient city of Jerusalem as the symbol and reality of our national life.

The sixteenth blessing, *Shema kolenu*, "hear our voice," asks for a compassionate response to our prayers: "Do not

turn us away empty-handed." Here, anyone can add a supplication for individual or general matters that were not mentioned earlier, and this ends the section of specific petitions.
As Psalm 102 says, "A prayer of the afflicted: ... Lord, hear
my prayer and my cry to you shall come."

Now we can combine the thirteen middle blessings
with the six opening and closing ones, to display the "necklace" of the *Shemoneh esreh*. We can see that with these
prayers, echoing the words of the prophets and psalmists,
we hear, speak, envision, and thus begin to embody within
ourselves a redemptive vision of the world.[52]

The Necklace of the Weekday Amidah

19. Bless us with kindness,
peace, light

1. God's saving acts

18B. Gratitude for acts
of redemption

2. God's power
for life

18A. Gratitude for
sustaining our lives

3. God's holiness

17. Restoring
holy service

16. Hear our prayer

4,5,6. Individual
inner dimensions:
discernment,
teshuvah,
forgiveness

14,15. Communal
outer dimensions:
Jerusalem,
Davidic kingship

7,8,9. Individual
outer dimensions:
help in our
struggles, healing,
sustenance

11,12,13.
Communal inner
dimensions:
justice, eliminating
evil, supporting
good

10. Sound the shofar
for our return

After saying the *Amidah*, we are invited to add a private prayer (not to be repeated by the *chazzan*) which begins, *Elohai n'tzor....* This prayer is quoted in the Talmud as having come from Mar ben Ravina, possibly a fifth century scholar, and is part of a list of individual scholars' prayers, many of which were incorporated into the siddur at various points. This particular prayer emphasizes once more the nullification of ego, reminding us that as we leave the ethereal world of the prayer service and go out to work in the world, we must continually put ego aside.

> Keep my tongue from evil and my lips from lies.
> And to those who would curse me, let my soul be
> silent, and like dust to everyone.
> Open my heart to your Torah; your mitzvot may my
> soul pursue.
> All those who plot evil against me, speedily annul
> their designs and frustrate their schemes.
> Act for the sake of Your Name, act for the sake of
> Your right hand [of compassion], act for the sake
> of Your holiness, act for the sake of Your Torah, to
> deliver your beloved ones: May your right hand
> save and answer me.

Then comes a quotation from Psalms 19:15 that has a mystical numerology: Ten words in Hebrew which contain ten "*yuds*," the tenth letter of the alphabet. The yud, which also refers to the world of Atzilut, symbolizes reaching to the innermost depths where the heart and mind connect to God. It says in English, "May the words of my mouth and the meditations of my heart be pleasing to you, Lord, my Rock and my Redeemer." Finally, a verse adapted from the book of Job is familiar to most Jews from the song, *Oseh shalom bimromav,*

namely: "May the One who brings peace in the heights
bring peace to us, and to all Israel; and let us say, 'Amen.'"

Speaking Silence

What do these prayers have to do with being in the fourth
world, the world of *Atzilut*? One might imagine it a world of
silence --but no, we speak. The human being's unique quality
is to be *medaber*, the Speaker. In Ezekiel's chariot vision, there
is a moment when the vision of God is appearing and he sees
something he describes as *chashmal* similar to a surrounding
fire. This mysterious word is identified in the Talmud as made
up of two words: *chash*, silence, and *mal*, speaking.[53] Mystics
understand this as a key to redemption. I will borrow from
the suggestion but make it simpler: The silent-speech of the
Amidah is the place where Godliness can appear or "emanate"
(in one of the meanings of *Atzilut*).

Of course, the *Amidah* is our petitioners' prayer, and in that
respect like the prayers of human beings universally. What makes
it different from ordinary petitioner prayers as they are usually
understood – "give us this day our daily bread" or "*El na refa na
lah*" (a prayer for healing) – is that we enter from a different perspective. We have been on a journey that prepared us.

If we have been successful in mining the potential of the
prayers, we are in a place of gratitude and joy; we are in love
with life. Our will has been transformed through gaining a
much larger perspective on the cosmos, and through commit-
ting to a covenant love relationship with God. We have a sense
of history, of enduring purpose.

Now, in the fourth scene, we are standing near (*etzel*), close
to God. In a sense, we can see the world from a divine view-

point. We hear through the prophets' words once again what are the divine concerns: to bring us close, forgive, advocate, heal, sustain, connect us, to teach us to love justice and goodness and to hate evil. We can imagine God somehow next to us, informing every cell and organ of our bodies, murmuring in the background, whispering in our ears. And we join in the scene by speaking the words, not only the written ones but also of our own needs and those of our community and people.

Abraham Joshua Heschel, the great Jewish poet-philosopher of the mid-twentieth century, wrote about the prophets in a unique way. He said they grasped the pathos of God. He adopted the word pathos from the Greek, meaning feeling. But it didn't mean just emotion, either – it is about what we could call feeling-consciousness. In contrast to the medieval philosophers who saw God as Absolute Intellect, Heschel experienced God as feeling-ful. Heschel was convinced that the philosophers, too much influenced by Islamic philosophy which in turn depended on the revival of Greek thought, had misled us. Jewish thought, in his view, rooted in a midrashic sensibility, was "anthropopathic". This means that God's responses cannot be equated with human emotions, but we definitely could not understand God without recognizing that those closest to him, the prophets and poets, felt God as angry, regretful, curious, yearning, joyful. They were aware of divine pathos, not only divine thought. Thus their speech was full of passion as well.

In reading the prophets, one can't escape the sense that they grasped the situations of which they spoke, the socio-political contexts, as a total feeling-thought experience, rich with imagery as well as with a sense of impending reality. They "foresaw," or perhaps "fore-felt" God's action, as they described what happened or would happen to the Jews and to other peoples, and also as they promised a future where there would be resolution, peace, blessedness. They foresaw the potential for good even in turbulent times – and knew that it was God who could bring that about. The people had only to align with that intent.

The prophets grasped how God felt, and gave articulation to that passion and empathy. At the same time, they turned, and we turn now, in compassion toward the world of *Asiyah*, where things happen, where lives are broken and in need of redemption. From the innermost reality, near to the heart of God, we relate to the most external world. Our sages were absolutely convinced that the cosmos tips toward goodness. More than tips: God saves, rescues. God is invested in human striving and thriving, offering help; we too can be invested in cosmic striving and thriving, the evolution of the cosmos from within.

To put this in other words: We know, without quite being able to define it, that holiness requires a transcendent perspective on the world. Yet, though we are a family of priests with a holy mission, like a family we need a home, communal structures, an organization of life; and that is where our work has to start. The *Shemoneh esreh* with its nineteen blessings expresses that dialectic between the transcendent and the ordinary – the holiness we cannot grasp, and the structures of individual and communal life that stubbornly remain our work. "Man goes out to his labor in the morning and returns in the evening." The necklace circles around to where it started, back to the world we know - but with a difference.

Chapter 6

Turning Outward

Walking away into normal life directly from the *Amidah* would not be easy. Additional prayers were recommended or became customary over the centuries. *Tachanun*, "supplications," provided a time for additional personal prayers, and communal prayers at times of distress were added as written sections, especially for Monday and Thursday which were customary fast days. A repetition of *Ashrei* and another *Kedushah* (beginning "A redeemer will come to Zion...) are in the traditional prayer book, as well as at least two slightly different versions of Kaddish, one in honor of our scholars and one or more led by mourners in the congregation. Various additional songs became customary in different traditions, particularly on Shabbat. A "psalm of the day" is usually said. All these ensure that people have the opportunity to pray for what they need, and that they feel supported by the congregation.

On Mondays and Thursdays and special days that can fall on weekdays (Rosh Chodesh, Hanukkah), a Torah reading follows *Tachanun*. Unlike the Shabbat reading which covers the entire weekly *parsha* divided into seven *aliyot* (portions for those "coming up" to the Torah), the Monday and Thursday readings are composed of three short *aliyot* to save time. The ritual chants are recited quickly, including the Torah portions that were used when the Jewish people, in the desert wanderings, rose up from their camping place and settled back down again (Bamidbar 10:35-36):

> And it came to pass, when the ark set forward, that
> Moses said: "Rise up, O Lord, and let Thine enemies
> be scattered; and let them that hate Thee flee before
> Thee." And when it rested, he said: "Return, O Lord,
> unto the ten thousands of myriads of Israel."

In a sense, the "setting forth" of the ark is like our taking the words of Torah and singing them to the world; while the "resting" is returning to our home, among our own people.

There is a kind of pilgrimage in this Torah ritual. The first of the two verses above, recognizable from a familiar *Kumah Adonai* melody, is joined with a verse from Isaiah: "For from Zion will the Torah come forth, and the word of Lord from Jerusalem." This takes us out of the desert and into the settled land of Israel. Then follows a rabbinic blessing: "Blessed is He who gave the Torah to His people Israel in His holiness." Wherever we are, when we take out the Torah, we are expressing our holy mission from God. The second verse from Bamidbar accompanies the act of putting the Torah away in the Ark, and is accompanied by several other verses as well. The feminine form here is referring to the Torah:

It is a tree of life for those who grasp her, and her supporters are happy. (Proverbs 3.18)
Her ways are ways of pleasantness and all her paths are peace. (Proverbs 3.17)

Bring us back to You, Lord, and we shall return; renew our days as of old. (Eichah 5:21)

Having read the Torah, we are finding happiness, peace, and renewal, and return to ourselves.

Aleinu

The final required prayer in all customs is the *Aleinu*, which in a way mirrors the *Mah Tovu* quoted at the beginning of this book. *Mah tovu* starts with a blessing from a non-Jewish prophet (Balaam from the book of Numbers/Bamidbar) and celebrates entering into the holy space of prayer, God's sanctuary. *Aleinu*, preceding our departure from the holy space, emphasizes our uniqueness and distinctiveness among the community of nations.

In the chart below, we can see several points of comparison and contrast. Both songs speak of bowing before God, but the *Aleinu* refers to God the King, where the *Mah tovu* names God more intimately as "my Maker." In *Aleinu* God is enthroned on high, His presence extending through the distant cosmos; in *Mah tovu* God is accessible in His "house," and the person praying expresses love for the place. The closing prayer addresses God manifested in "strength", the opening prayer addresses His "kindness." Again we are reminded of the way *Ashrei* and other prayers alternate or pair expressions of "greatness" with those of "goodness."

ALEINU	MAH TOVU
It is on us—*Aleinu* – to praise the Lord of All, to ascribe greatness to the Molder of Creation	
Who has us not made us like the nations of the lands. nor placed us like the families of the earth, or made our portion like theirs, nor our destiny like all their multitudes.	How good are your tents, Yaakov, And your dwelling places, Israel!
We bend and bow and acknowledge	And I – through Your abundant kindness I will enter Your house; I will bow toward Your holy sanctuary
Before the King, King of kings, the Holy One Blessed Be He.	in awe of You.
Who extends the heavens and establishes the earth and sits honored in heaven above	Lord, I love the house where You reside,
and the Presence of His strength is in the highest heights.	the dwelling place of Your glory.
	And I – I will bow, and kneel, and bend
He is our God, there is no other.	before the Lord my Maker.
Truly our King, none but Him – as it is written in His Torah "You shall know today, and take it to heart, that the Lord is God in the heavens above and on the earth below – there is no other."	
Thus we hope to you, Lord our God	And I – my prayer is to You, Lord at a time of desire --
to see soon the beauty of your strength	God, in Your abundant kindness
to remove idolatry from the earth and false gods be cut off, to perfect the earth as the kingdom of the Almighty.	answer me in the truth of Your salvation.

The *Aleinu* continues with a larger statement about God's kingship, including verses from Tanakh:

> And all mortals will call in Your name to cause to turn to
> you all the wicked of the earth. They will recognize and
> know – all the inhabitants of the earth – that to You
> every knee should bend, every tongue should swear.
> Be- fore You Lord our God they will bend and cast
> themselves down and to the glory of Your name they
> will give homage; and they will receive all together
> the yoke of Your kingship and You will reign over them
> soon, eternally. For the kingdom is Yours and for eter-
> nity You will reign in glory, as it is written in Your Torah
> (Exod 15.18) "The Lord will reign forever." And it is said
> (Zech 14.9) "And the Lord will be king over all the earth;
> on that day it will be: the Lord one and His name one."

Nevertheless, there is a strong symmetry between these two beautiful pieces, opening and closing with deep affirmation, an awareness of our relationship to God and divine redemption.

Clearly, *Mah tovu* is a personal prayer, as indicated by the repeated *V'ani*, "and I," while the *Aleinu* is plural, "we." But also the *Aleinu* claims for the Jewish people a vision that extends beyond our communities and *klal Yisrael*, namely a time when all the nations will accept the kingship of God, as the praying community has just done in the *Shema*. As we "bend and bow and acknowledge," they will eventually "bend and cast themselves down and...give homage." The "truth of Your salvation" (*b'emet yishecha*) for an individual in *Mah tovu* has been expanded to *tikun olam b'malchut Shaddai*, the "correction (or perfecting) of the world as a kingdom of the Almighty."

On that last point, the name of God used here is that which God, in talking to Moses at the Burning Bush, identified as an older name: "Your ancestors knew me as *El Shaddai*," but to Moses and the enslaved Hebrews, God would be known by a new name. The *Aleinu* with *"malkhut Shaddai"* seems to be deliberately pointing to a name from pre-history, before the shaping of the Jewish people as they are known today. Its most pressing message is that the false gods and idolatries that have arisen over centuries must be discarded, "cut off," uprooted, so that the ancient and future message of oneness can become a reality.

Further, it is *aleinu*, on us, an obligation we take on as we leave the place of prayer, that we become the witnesses daily to the divine Oneness. *Ein od*, "there is no other." One meaning is that there are no other deities. Another, more radical reading is: *efes zulato* – there is nothing except Him; and *ein od* –there is no other reality at all. As the mystics say, *Ein Sof*, the Endless, the Infinite. We live in the infinite reality that is God.

We come to God in the morning, asking to be shown the divine reality in the world. We leave our time of prayer able to affirm, on notes of certainty as the climax of our prayers, that there will be a time when that vision will be reality for all.

Appendix 1
Structure of Weekday Shacharit

Mah tovu (sometimes said after morning blessings)

A. *Bircot HaShachar*, Morning Blessings
    a. Over body, soul, Torah
    b. Over gifts we have received of abilities and functions

B. *Pesukei d'Zimrah*, Verses of Song
    a. *Baruch She'amar* and opening blessing
        i. Songs of offerings
            1. *Ashrei* & Psalm 145
        ii. Songs of processional (Halleluyahs)
    b. Blessing of thanks (preliminary conclusion)
        i. Donations of gifts
        ii. Second temple
    c. *Yishtabach* / concluding blessing

C. *Barchu* (call to prayer)

D. *Shema* and Its Blessings
    a. *Yotzer Or*, creation of light including *kedushah*
        i. *Ahavah Rabbah*, love
            1. *Shema*, 3 paragraphs
        ii. *Emet v'yatziv*, truth
    b. Ge'ulah, creation of a people including a "hidden" *kedushah*
        Note: *Emet v'yatziv* and *Ge'ulah* are considered one blessing

E. *Amidah* or *Shemoneh esreh*
    a. *Avot* / God's saving acts
    b. *Gevurot* / God giving life
    c. *Kedushah* / God's holiness
        a. 3 Individual / inner dimensions
        b. 3 individual / outer dimensions
        c. 3 communal / inner dimensions
        d. 2 communal / outer dimensions
            i. ALL VOICES (Shema kolenu)
    d. *Retzeh*: Holiness of sanctuary / priesthood
    e. *Modim* I: Thanks for sustaining our life
      Modim II: Thanks for salvations (Hanukkah, Purim etc)
    f. *Shalom*: Blessing for Peace to "seal all the blessings"

Additional prayers, Torah reading,

Aleinu, Mourners' Kaddish

Appendix 2
Meditations for Prayer in the Four Worlds

On the next few pages are suggestions for contemplative meditations that may help to orient you toward the "scene" and intent of the prayers within each of the four main sections of weekday *Shacharit*. In the form presented here, the idea is to have a focus at the beginning, then mix them in with the prayers. After some experimentation, you may adapt them in ways that will work for you.

The World of Asiyah

Before saying the Morning Blessings, spend a few moments contemplating your being in the physical world.

Imagine yourself standing outside a courtyard with three gates in sequence ahead of you. These represent Body, Soul, and Mind/Torah. As you read the appropriate blessings for each, watch its gate open and see yourself walking through.

Now you stand before a small clear pool, into which you can look as if in a mirror, seeing your entire self, top to bottom, and feel yourself as a body.

Imagine that a fountain comes up from that pool and spreads a fine, warm mist up and over you, which gently comes down upon you as you say the first seven *brachot*.

Touch each part of your body lightly as you say the blessings over:

- distinguishing day and night / brain/head
- opening the eyes / eyes
- clothing the naked / torso
- freeing the bound / arms
- raising the bowed / knees
- spreading earth over waters / soles (feel ground)
- providing all my needs / feet/shoes

Now feel the earth beneath your feet, and imagine your body filling from below upward, with warmth and energy from the earth, as you say the remaining blessings:

- making firm my steps / feet (moving)
- girding Israel with strength / torso
- crowning Israel with glory / head or tefillin
- giving strength to weary/all
- breaking the bonds of sleep / eyes
- attaching me to good, keeping me far from evil / heart.

The World of Yetzirah

Take a moment to center yourself. Then imagine yourself walking up a slope toward an awesome temple, a journey you have been yearning to make for a long time. You have awakened in the morning with great joy and vitality, feeling as though your troubles are over. Your steps are light, rhythmic. You feel thankful that you can at last bring an offering, a gift to God in thanks for your life as it is this very day.

As you approach the temple, the altar has a bright aura around it, almost a flame. You sense a depth of presence here that you have never felt before. Sit or stand quietly. Allow the feeling to arise in you that you could stay here happily forever.

Quietly say: *Ashrei yoshvei veitecha....*

After some moments of contemplation, you turn (physically if you wish, or with your inner eye) and see a crowd of pilgrims joining you from below. They walk in groups, from different towns, from the guilds, from the villages, each with their own unique character. Songs arise from their hearts and you hum along. A company of soldiers joins them; groups of young people; elders slowly bring up the rear. As they come close, the instrumentalists of the temple choir appear.

See now the Levites taking their places on the temple staircase and sing the beautiful songs of the sacrifice.
Recite any of the verses you wish, culminating in Halleluyah!
Recite the *brachah* of *Yishtabach*, and meditate for a few moments on the phrase, "Life of the Worlds."

The World of Beriah

You are seated on a grassy meadow on a hill or, if you prefer, on a dune or rocky crag overlooking the ocean. It is before the first light of dawn, and stars still are visible in the western sky. As you turn to the east, you see a faint light. Breathe slowly. In your mind's eye, streaks of sunlight begin to paint the horizon with pink and orange.

Breathe a few more times. Imagine the world waking up – deer coming to drink at a stream, squirrels running through the trees, birds in flight.

Wind, rain, sun, all the possibilities of a new day.

Say the first line of the *brachah, Yotzer Or*, and then recite, *How many are your works, O Lord! In wisdom You have made them all.*

Allow your own imagination to guide you through the cosmos, whether to the vast expanses of space, the depths of the sea, or the micro-worlds of molecules, atoms, photons.

Do you hear any sounds? Let the experience of sound or silence fill your awareness.

Blessed are You, Lord, who forms the luminaries – *yotzer hame'orot.*

Now go inside, feeling your own heart and its vibrations throughout your body, Let your breathing become deep and allow your chest muscles to expand. Imagine your heart opening slowly to receive love.

Call up a memory from your personal past of when you felt supported and loved in your learning, or in a project you cared about. A teacher, a parent, a group of friends were intensely part of this with you; or perhaps someone inspired and encouraged you or helped you overcome an obstacle.

Remember how that felt, how good it is to be seen, understood, supported.

Say quietly, *Ahavah rabbah.*

Recognize that you can create that feeling any time you wish.

Know, in that moment, that you are unique in the world.

Now see yourself joining with the Jewish people, coming to stand with them at Sinai, listening with them in the desert, now and forever.

Shema Yisrael, Adonai Elohenu, Adonai Echad.

You are ready for anything now – to cross the sea with them, to climb a mountain; you are bound together now and forever.

The World of Atzilut

A personal *Amidah*

"Open my lips, O Adonai"...

What do your lips say about their current state of being?

Are they warm or cool, relaxed or fidgety, dry or moist, closed or open?

What do your hands say? Your feet? Your stomach? Your muscles?

Check out the various parts of your body and see if they have anything to say, and whether they are willing to allow your mouth to speak for them.

Ask your heart, noticing the area around the heart as well.

Look around. Does anything in your environment want you to speak for it?

How about your family? Friends? People far away?

Close your eyes and ask your heart to take you to some person or persons

or other kinds of beings who need you to speak for them.

Stay with them awhile, gently watching them with your mind's eye and feeling toward them with your heart;

then speak what they want you to say.

Give thanks for the opportunity to speak for yourself and others.

"Hear our prayer, *Adonai*...

Bless us all together, as one, with the Light of Your Face...

As you create peace in all the worlds, grant peace to us on earth."

Sit for a few moments in silence.

Appendix 3

**Historical Outline
of Events and Periods Relevant to the Weekday Liturgy**

Year
B.C.E.
586 -- Destruction of First Temple; Babylonian exile.
    No known communal liturgy other than Temple rites.
516 -- Beginning of return from Exile. Persian rule. Many remain
in Babylon.

- Second Temple is constructed. Besides the sacrifices, Levites sang Psalms (hymns), but we do not know specifics,
  other than possibly a psalm for each day of the week.

458 -- Ezra the Priest, also known as the Scribe (*HaSofer*) recon-
structs Jewish life in Israel. Nehemiah is governor, still under the
rule of Persia.

- *Anshei Knesset HaGedolah* (Men of the Great Assembly)
  is formed in this era.

- Torah readings are prescribed, at least for holidays, possibly on certain special Shabbats.

- Some blessings were prescribed, probably including *Kid-
  dush* and *Havdalah*.

- It is not clear whether Torah readings were done only in
  Jerusalem or in other communities as well.

- We have no written records, so these statements about liturgical development in this period are inferences based
  on a variety of later sources.

333 -- Alexander the Great conquers the land of Israel and vast
territories all the way to India. Greek influence spreads throughout the Mediterranean area.

300 -- Ben Sira: at some point in the late 3rd century a book of wisdom (later called in Latin "Ecclesiasticus," not the same as Ecclesiastes) circulated. It includes examples of prayer, some of which may have been similar in content to *Amidah*. However, Ben Sira does not use the *"Baruch ata..."* formula of Rabbinic Judaism.

180? -- Community formed at Qumran in early second century B.C.E., a separatist community that opposed the priesthood in Jerusalem and was itself probably led by priests. We know about this community from the Dead Sea Scrolls found in the 20th century; they may have been the part of a group called "Essenes" by others; but that is not what they called themselves. This community had extensive liturgies including weekday prayers, a somewhat different calendar but with all the Jewish festivals, *Rosh Chodesh*, and Shabbat.

* n.d. *Mishmarot.* A rotation of temple priests was established, so that each priest would serve two weeks of the year; the rest of the year he would be in his home community. Some think this custom may go all the way back to the time of Ezra.

* n.d. *Maamadot.* At the Temple in Jerusalem, a custom arose of having lay representatives from outlying communities join the priests at the Temple to observe and possibly bring korbanot (sacrifices) from their communities.

* n.d. *"Shema* liturgy." The priests recited *Shema* and other Torah passages along with certain prayers; see chapter 3. This is known from a description in the Mishnah which was written down much later, around 200 C.E.

165-140 -- Maccabeean war against the Syrian/Greek rulers of Israel. Independent Jewish rule began. However, the priesthood was contested and internal struggles continued for many years.

- Sectarian groups including Pharisees and Sadducees become known by those names. Pharisees transmitted the tradition later called "rabbinic Judaism."

63 -- Romans conquered the land of Israel.

C.E. (Common Era dating begins)

0-40 (approx.) -- time of Hillel and Shammai

40 -- "Jesus movement" or "Nazarene movement" appears – what will later become Christianity (death of Jesus was probably 29 C.E.).

66-70 -- First Jewish Revolt against Rome. Temple is destroyed in 70 C.E.

- Torah study is re-established in an academy at Yavneh (near modern Tel Aviv). Title of "rabbi" becomes more common.

90 -- Under the leadership of Rabban Gamliel, the *Amidah* is established as an obligatory prayer, at least in the academies.

90-200 -- Competition with Christianity is intense in some regions of the Mediterranean.

132-135 -- Second Jewish Revolt under Bar Kochba. Rome wins and razes Jerusalem. Many leave and join the community that still exists in Babylon.

200 -- The Mishnah is edited and becomes the basis for Jewish law.

- Rabbinic influence grows over Jewish communities in Israel, Babylon and elsewhere.
- Christianity, which had been a small competing sect in the second century, nearly dies out in the land of Israel, but spreads widely in the rest of the Mediterranean.

200-400 -- Liturgical development includes the practice of Morning Blessings (at home) and *Pesukei d'Zimrah* as a prelude to the *Shema* liturgy.

380 -- Christianity becomes the official religion of the Roman Empire.

400 -- The Talmud of the Land of Israel (*Yerushalmi*) is completed.
476 -- Rome falls to barbarian rule; Christianity in the East (Byzantine empire) becomes the dominant force in Israel and Babylonia.
500 -- The Talmud of the Babylonian community (*Bavli*) is completed. Beginning shortly after this time, we know of many poets who were writing piyyutim, liturgical poems for the various liturgies. Such compositions have come down from earlier centuries too, but from this time on many of the paytanim (composers) are known by name. Jewish practice for the next several centuries included the chanting of many kinds of poems, designed to embellish and enrich particular parts of our prayer services.
632 -- Islamic armies conquer Israel and Babylonia.
700 -- Karaite sect grows – believing only in the written Torah, rejecting the oral tradition of the rabbis, and praying only with the book of Psalms.
ca. 850 -- First written prayer book, that of Amram, head of a yeshiva in Babylonia; it is closer to Sephardic than to Ashkenazic rite.

For subsequent developments, see:
http://opensiddur.org/wp-content/uploads/2010/05/
Aharon-Varady-NuspercentE1percentB8percentA-
5aot-Tree-3.5.4.pdf

Suggested Readings

The list below offers the student of prayer an entry into a few recent interpretations, historical expositions, and approaches to invigorate Jewish prayer. Each of these can lead the student into further resources and applications. The dates refer to hard copy versions; recent editions of some of these are available in e-book (such as Kindle) format.

- Reuven Hammer, *Entering Jewish Prayer: A Guide to Personal Devotion and the Worship Service*. New York: Schocken Books, 1994.
- Lawrence A. Hoffman, *The Way Into Jewish Prayer*. Woodstock, VT: Jewish Lights, 2000.
- _____. *The Art of Jewish Prayer: Not for Clergy Only*. Woodstock, VT: Skylight Paths, 1999.
- _____. *My People's Prayer Book: Traditional Prayers, Modern Commentaries*. 10 volumes, each on a different section of prayers. Woodstock, VT: Jewish Lights, 1997-2013.
- Kimelman, Reuven, "The Shema' Liturgy: From Covenant Ceremony to Coronation," in J. Tabory (ed), *Kenishta: Studies in Synagogue Life*, (Ramat Gan, 2001), pp. 9-105.
- _____. *The Rhetoric of the Jewish Prayer Book*. Oxford: Littman Library of Jewish Civilization, forthcoming in 2017.
- Prager, Marcia. *The Path of Blessing: Experiencing the Energy and Abundance of the Divine*. Woodstock, VT: Jewish Lights, paperback 2003.

About the Author

Tamar Frankiel, PhD., is Professor of Comparative Religion at the Academy for Jewish Religion, California, where she also has served as President and Provost. She has taught liturgy, ritual studies, and modern Jewish history, and has also held positions in Religious Studies at Stanford, Princeton, Claremont School of Theology and the University of California.

As an exponent of significant issues in modern Jewish life, she is the author of *The Voice of Sarah: Feminine Spirituality and Traditional Judaism; The Gift of Kabbalah; Kabbalah: A Brief Introduction for Christians*, and co-author with Cantor Judy Greenfeld of *Minding the Temple of the Soul and Entering the Temple of Dreams*.

Her doctorate is from the University of Chicago in the field of History of Religions, with a specialty in modern Christianity and religion in America. In that field, she is the author of a widely-used textbook on Christianity and two works on nineteenth century American religion, *Gospel Hymns and Social Religion* and *California's Spiritual Frontiers*.

Notes

1. The *Mah tovu* prayer is sung or said when entering a synagogue to pray. If you are praying in private, it is said before beginning the main series of morning blessings (after putting on *tallit* and *tefillin*, if you wear them). I do not discuss *tallit* or *tefillin* ("phylacteries") here because I have no personal practice with them. Good sources are Aryeh Kaplan's books, *Tefillin*, and *Tzitzith: A Thread of Light* (Orthodox Union, NCSY, 1993).

2. In Buddhism this is called the "chain of causation" or "interdependent origination," classically regarded as having twelve stages. The most relevant ones for a comparison with the kabbalistic World of Action are: grasping, adoption, becoming [something]: "The eighth link of grasping is involved with wanting or avoiding something and this leads to the ninth link of adoption in which one makes definite plans to get the object of our desire or to eliminate or avoid something we have deemed unpleasant. In the tenth link, this decision is put into action." Thrangu Rinpoche, "Twelve Links of Interdependent Origination," from a 2001 book published by Namo Buddha Publications. Access online at http://www.rinpoche.com/teachings/12links.pdf. This bringing into actuality is what creates karma (which also means action) and leads to rebirth, in Buddhist philosophy.

3. For a discussion of the midrashic background of the Priestly Blessing, see Tamar Frankiel and Judy Greenfeld, *Entering the Temple of Dreams* (Woodstock, VT: Jewish Lights, 2000), chapter 5.

4. For more detailed study, see Stephen R. Schach, *The Structure of the Siddur* (Northvale, NJ: Jason Aronson, 1996). This book is out of print but may be available in a library or from a used book vendor.

5. Rabbi Sacks discusses this on page xxiii of the Introduction to the Koren Siddur. Rabbi Dr. Jacob Milgrom uses a very similar image in his book on Leviticus, where he calls the structure a "ring"

with a "latch." See "The Structure of Leviticus," in *Leviticus* (Continental Commentaries), Augsburg Fortress e-books, 2004. I use the term "necklace" as it suggests a flexible oval rather than a fixed circle. The use of chiasmus in the *Shema* liturgy has been highlighted by Rabbi Dr. Reuven Kimelman: with the *Shema* blessings, "a linear reading must give way to a chiastic one." See "The Shema' Liturgy: From Covenant Ceremony to Coronation," in J. Tabory (ed), *Kenishta: Studies in Synagogue Life*, (Ramat Gan, 2001), pp. 9-105; the discussion of chiastic structure begins on p.25.

     6. For some simple examples of chiasmus, check the definition in Wikipedia: http://en.wikipedia.org/wiki/Chiasmus. There, we see it in classical literature and Shakespeare. It also appears in our biblical tradition. One of the great twentieth century biblical commentators Nechama Liebovitz, following Martin Buber, noted examples in the story of the building of the *Mishkan*, the portable wilderness tabernacle.

     7. The blessings over body, soul, and Torah are a rich source of spiritual study in themselves. Please refer to Tamar Frankiel and Cantor Judy Greenfeld: *Minding the Temple of the Soul* (Jewish Lights, 1997).

     8. Access online at: http://www.come-and-hear.com/berakoth/berakoth_60.html.

     9. The Ashkenaz siddur places the blessings right after "distinguishing day and night," but other traditions differ in their placement. Adding these three would "mirror" the blessings for body, soul, and Torah that were said at the outset, making 21 blessings in all. See page 57 for the numerological significance of 21.

     10. Rabbi Aryeh Kaplan discussed the connection between music and prophecy – the primary example of inspiration in our early history, and the model for much of later mysticism – in his *Inner Space: Introduction to Kabbalah, Meditation, and Prophecy*, edited by Abraham Sutton (Jerusalem: Moznaim Books, 1990), pp. 149, 225 n.118.

     11. See Rabbi Elie Munk, *World of Prayer* (NY: Philip Feldheim, 1953), vol. 1: *Daily Prayers*, p. 60.

12. Jewish numerology, called *gematria*, has many systems, but the simplest is that each letter of the *alef-bet* is assigned a number in order, so that *alef* = 1, *beit* = 2, etc up to *yud* = 10, then the next letter *chaf* = 20, etc until 90, then *kaf* = 100, to the last letter *tav* = 400. Every word and phrase can thus be calculated as a number; and relationships of words can be established based on their having the same number.

13. The most common reason given is that David, as a warrior who had shed blood, was not the appropriate person to build the Temple (1 Chronicles 28:3).

14. Today, our custom is to say a prayer of thanksgiving – *bircat hagomel* – after the Torah reading but while the Torah is still out of the ark, for having safely come through (1) a serious illness or childbirth, (2) having been in prison, (3) crossing an ocean or (4) crossing a desert. Other life-threatening situations may be included as well such as being saved from robbers or terrorists, auto or construction accidents.

15. As Rabbi Munk points out, there are twenty occurrences of the Tetragrammaton, and the one occurrence in which the 4-letter name is encoded: *Yismechu Hashamayim V'tagel Ha-aretz* – a 4-word verse with the 4 letters. In *gematria*, the number 21 is the equivalent of the Divine Name *Ehyeh, alef-heh-yud-heh*, "I will be." When Moshe encountered God at the burning bush and asked his name, God said *Ehyeh asher Ehyeh*, "I will be what I will be." This was Moshe's encounter with God's glory, an ephiphany of fire in the bush – and here, the song of 21 names alludes to God's glory and fire coming down on the sacrifices.

16. Many biblical commentators, including Nechamah Liebowitz and Samson Rafael Hirsch have noted the parallels between divine creation and the *Mishkan*.

17. This psalm has been beautifully analyzed by Rabbi Reuven Kimelman, and it should be read in his original. See http://www.myjewishlearning.com/article/ashrei-pslam-145/

18. The passage is also important to the mystical tradition because of its terminology; it is understood to contain references to the "seven lower sefirot" identified later in *Kabbalah*: "Yours, Lord, are the greatness and the power, the glory, majesty and splendor..." *ha-gedulah, v'ha-gevurah, v'ha-tiferet, v'ha-netzach, v'ha-hod,* where *gedulah* is an alternate term for *chesed*. It continues, "For all in heaven and earth is yours," and "all" (*chol*) refers to the *sefirah yesod*. "Yours is the dominion" is considered to refer to the *sefirah malkhut*.

19. It is possible that the response *Baruch Hu* might have, at one time, occurred after every phrase or line, with *Baruch Shmo* signaling the end of the series. (Note: "Call and response" in was a common Jewish way of reciting or singing many prayers, even long after *siddurim* became readily available. It can have an energetic effect on congregations today as well.)

20. Munk, *World of Prayer* I, 87. Rabbi Sacks translates, "Giver of Life to the worlds." Many translators use "eternal God," because *olamim*, the masculine plural of *olam*, usually refers to times, i.e. eternity; whereas *olamot*, the feminine plural, refers to worlds in spatial terms (although the "Four Worlds," *arba olamot*, are not exactly spaces in the normal sense). The phrase *Chei Ha-Olamim* could also be translated, "life of the generations," because olam sometimes refers to people in community. The phrase as such does not appear in the Bible, but we have *tzur ha-olamim* (eternal rock, as in Rock of Ages), and malchut *kol-olamim* (kingdom of all times or all worlds). Given the context of *Pesukei d'Zimrah*, where the praise of God comes from all beings as well as eternally, and following Rabbi Munk's gloss, I use "Life of the Worlds," intending to include time and space. In either translation, it is a distinctive phrase for this section of prayer.

21. Here are some examples of the many words in Hebrew. With the tone of joy or gratitude: *hallel, shevach, tehillah,* all meaning praise (*Halleluyah! Yishtabach, Tehillim*); *shirah, zemer,* and *rinah,* all meaning song; *hoda'ah,* meaning thanks (*todah* is the familiar form). Words indicating prayer, not necessarily with joy, are *tefillah* (from

the word *hitpallel*, literally to judge oneself or examine oneself), *hodayah*, confession or acknowledgment (*Modeh ani*, the waking prayer), *bevakashah*, pleading; *tachnun*, supplication, which is the title of a section of prayer after the *Amidah* for weekdays.

22. The name "*Yah*" has been proclaimed many times in the "*halleluyahs*" that precede this ending prayer. Indeed, there were eleven halleluyahs in the last six Psalms as beginning and ending markers. Eleven added to fifteen is twenty-six, which is the *gematria* of the four letter name of God.

23. We do not know when this selection took place, but most believe that the oldest parts of the formal liturgy developed between the exile to Babylon and Ezra's leadership of the returned exiles, that is, between the mid-sixth and mid-fifth century B.C.E. The *Shema* recital and that of the Ten Commandments, were undoubtedly among the earliest. Some scholars believe that the third paragraph of the *Shema* was added later.

24. For more detail on the *Shema* recital and the individual paragraphs, there are many commentaries, which I will not replicate or summarize here. Please see the essays in *My People's Prayer Book: Traditional Prayers, Modern Commentaries* Vol 1: The *Sh'ma* and Its Blessings, edited by Rabbi Lawrence Hoffman (Woodstock, VT: Jewish Lights, 1997), and Norman Lamm's *Shema: Spirituality and Law in Judaism* (Philadelphia: Jewish Publication Society, 2000).

A good source for information on the return of previously "lost" communities to Judaism and to Israel is the website of Shavei Israel, shavei.org/communities. A sample: Bnei Menashe from India, Beta Israel from Ethiopia, Bnei Anousim from Spanish-speaking countries, Kaifeng Jews from China, Subotnik (Sabbath-keeping) Jews from Siberia, hidden Jews of Poland.

25. The premise of an evil deity parallel to a good one was a significant theological belief that the rabbis repeatedly battled. Zoroastrianism in Persia since the fifth century B.C.E., and Gnostic sects that sprang up around the time of Christianity, 2nd-4th centuries C.E., were major influences in spreading this belief.

26. One of the more remarkable examples of creative Talmudic thought in this area is in the tractate Chagigah, where the sages discuss processes of creation and the heavenly spheres. In a statement that seems to anticipate the idea of an expanding universe, Rav Yehudah said, "At the time that the Holy One, blessed be He, created the heaven and the earth, it went on expanding like two spools of cloth, until the Holy One rebuked it and brought it to a standstill" (B. Chagigah 12a).

27. Jon Levenson, *Creation and the Persistence of Evil: The Jewish Drama of Divine Omnipotence*, (Princeton University Press, 1994), pp. 53ff.

28. Munk, *World of Prayer* I, pp. 106-107.

29. The parallel acclamations of God's greatness and God's goodness may remind us of Rabbi Kimelman's analysis of Psalm 145 (*Ashrei*), and may be intended to echo that psalm.

30. Jon Levenson in his recent work, *The Love of God: Divine Gift, Human Gratitude, and Mutual Faithfulness in Judaism* (Princeton University Press, 2016), pp. 24-25, observes that *chesed* was used in the sense of loyalty, or covenantal love, in biblical times; so we may not be going to a larger concept but linking to essentially the same concept in the next *brachah*, depending on whether we read this as more the biblical or the later rabbinic meaning of *chesed*.

31. The Mishnah was compiled around 200 C.E.; the Second Temple had been destroyed in 70 C.E., but information about it was passed down through oral tradition. Rabbi Reuven Hammer has argued that, while this account probably indicates the framework that future liturgy would use, the first (unnamed) blessing was probably a general call to prayer or acclamation of God, not one of the blessings that later appear around the *Shema*. See "What Did They Bless? A Study of Mishnah Tamid 5:1," *Jewish Quarterly Review* 81 (1991), 302-24; and further discussion below.

32. The two blessings are also quite different in structure and tone, as you will see in our analyses. The *Yotzer Or* with its interest in God's glory and the heavenly hosts has a priestly tone, which makes

it more likely that it came from the Temple tradition. But this does not firmly establish a date. For the distinction between patriarchal/ priestly and scribal traditions, see Tzvee Zahavy, "The Politics of Piety: Social Conflict and the Emergence of Rabbinic Liturgy," accessible online at http://www.tzvee.com/Home/the-politics-of-piety.

33. We often think of Christianity splitting off from Judaism right after the death of Jesus or with the apostle Paul, but the separation wasn't so rapid or very clear. Jews who believed the "Jesus message" were still in synagogues and practiced Judaism as they had before; the main external distinction from mainstream Jews was that they held extra meetings on the first day of the week, Sunday. But it wasn't until the end of the first century that they were distinct enough to show up in the Roman records, in the form of disputes in court as to who was a Jew versus who was a Christian – and therefore did they have to pay the tax to support the emperor? (Jews were exempt as an "ancestral religion"; Christians were claiming they should be too.) It was not until the Christian church's Council of Nicaea in 325 C.E. that the church separated its calendar from that of the Jews, deciding how to figure the date of Easter on its own.

34. The new theological emphasis received additional promotion from a famous Christian heretic also from Asia Minor, named Marcion. Even though he was declared a heretic and excommunicated, he wielded influence for some time, as a wealthy person and son of a bishop. Marcion declared that the "old testament" prophecies were historical but did not refer to Jesus, who was bringing a higher message; and that the Jewish God was a god of wrath while Christianity preached a god of love. Joseph Tyson, "Anti-Judaism in Marcion and His Opponents," Studies in Jewish-Christian Relations (2006), https:// ejournals.bc.edu/ojs/index.php/scjr/article/download/1359/1269.

However, we should be clear that antisemitism was not an official doctrine; indeed, there was no unified Christian church at this time to propagate a doctrine. But there were anti-Jewish messages in Christian literature.

35. It is noteworthy that in this same period, Jewish communities stopped saying the Ten Commandments (as the priestly ceremony had done) because, according to the Talmud, the Christians were claiming it as theirs, the only Torah that was necessary. Dropping the commandments' recital also brought the focus to the *Shema*, and its words of love and concern. The other key part of the recital of the Ten Commandments, "I am the God who brought you out of Egypt" does appear in the *Shema* paragraphs as well.

36. Levenson's *Love of God* discusses at length these different models of love in the Hebrew Bible, demonstrating that the idea of love is multi-dimensional, rarely sentimental, but deeply passionate. Of course, love from parent to child can parallel the teacher/student relationship, since the parent is often a teacher. And vice-versa: for rabbinic Judaism, "anyone who teaches his friend's children Torah is considered as if he gave birth to them" (Sanhedrin 19a).

37. Kimelman, "The Shema' Liturgy: From Covenant Ceremony to Coronation," in J. Tabory (ed), *Kenishta: Studies in Synagogue Life*, (Ramat Gan, 2001), full citation in note 5. , pp. 9-105.

38. See n.46, and the discussion by Jon Levenson in the *Restoration of Israel: The Ultimate Victory of the God of Life* (New Haven, CT: Yale University Press, 2008).

39. See Koren Siddur, Ashkenaz, p. xxvi. With this comparison, Rabbi Sacks nicely resolves the tension between spontaneous and fixed prayer, which is recorded as far back as Talmudic times (see B. Berachot 29b). Of course, any Jew can pray on his own at any time, and various groups have advocated setting aside separate times for meditation and prayer outside the formal prayer. Communal prayer is required, to the extent that some prayers such as the *Barchu, Kedushah,* and *Kaddish*, as well as the Torah reading, cannot be said without a minyan (quorum of ten). Thus a person should feel obligated to "make a minyan" so that the community is not without their collective voice.

40. The composition of the *Amidah* in close to its current form – and thus the grounding of the *brachot* in the prophets - is attribut-

ed to Rabban Gamliel and his academy in the late first century CE, after the destruction of the Temple. While our tradition presumes that the *Amidah* came from earlier versions, scholars have not found any evidence of a daily version corresponding to this. Some think that the beginning and ending blessings have earlier antecedents, particularly because the Mishnah as noted before connected blessings with a priestly recital of *Shema*. Shabbat or holiday prayers (of which we also do not have texts) may have provided precedents. But this is most likely a new rendition, including requests that one universally finds in prayers, such as for sustenance or healing; concepts based in Jewish theology like pleas for forgiveness and *teshuvah*, and concerns of the community such as return from exile and rebuilding the city and nation.

Notably, the richest source we have for previous Jewish prayers, the scrolls of the Qumran community at the Dead Sea, shows no evidence of an *Amidah* though there are many other precedents such as *yotzer* prayers and extensive use of psalms (Rabbi Dr. Lawrence Schiffman, private conversation).

41. Since ancient times, rabbinic scholars have presented different interpretations of the structure. Among modern scholars, Rabbi Reuven Kimelman has already reviewed much of the earlier scholarship, and I am indebted to his insights from teachings at CLAL, particularly on some of the middle blessings (this analysis is no longer publicly available on the internet). Rabbi Elie Munk, former chief rabbi of France, inspired me from the beginning of my liturgical studies with his poetic and philosophical analysis in his two-volume *The World of Prayer*; full citation in note 11, cited earlier.

42. The number 13 probably varied in ancient times, and the total, with 6 beginning and ending blessings, contradicts the title, *Shemoneh esreh* or "18," where we now have 19. The mirroring of beginning and ending blessings is discussed by Rabbi Sacks in his introduction to the Koren Siddur, p. xxiv, and he traces it to Rabbi Joseph Soloveitchik.

43. Students of liturgy often learn the midrashic interpretation of the repetition of God before each patriarch's name – that it in-

dicates each ancestor experienced God differently – otherwise we could simply say "God of Abraham, Isaac, and Jacob." While this is a beautiful midrash, it contributes to the elision of the source in Exodus. Few teachers of liturgy have noted the importance of the biblical references in the first blessing. See, however, Rabbi Elie Kaunfer, "Prayer in Dialogue with Tanakh: A Novel Approach to Tefillah Education," *Hayidion: The Ravsak Journal*, accessed at https://ravsak.org/prayer-dialogue-tanakh-novel-approach-tefillah-education, February 28, 2016. Kaunfer notes that it is Rabbi Reuven Kimelman who emphasized that the liturgy is always in dialogue with biblical text, as is exemplified in "The Shema Liturgy" cited earlier.

44. This is in the fourth paragraph of blessing in *Bircat Hamazon*. As the Koren siddur indicates in the footnote (p.191), the tradition about this blessing is that it was composed by the teachers at Yavneh, expressing gratitude to God for preserving the bodies of those slaughtered by the Romans at Betar, the scene of the last battle of the Bar Kochba war in 135. One expression of "good" was for preserving the bodies, another for making it possible that they could be buried (Berachot 48b). It is astonishing that the sages found a place for gratitude in their hearts after the terrible defeat, which also left their community at Yavneh in tatters.

45. This is discussed at length, with great insight, by Levenson in his book referenced earlier, *Resurrection and the Restoration of Israel*. As the title indicates, Levenson makes a striking point when he explains that the ancients understood life and death as ends of a spectrum, not absolute opposites. For us, someone very ill or critically wounded is still alive until they are medically dead; certainly someone in captivity is fully alive. Question marks arise in conditions of extended coma or "vegetative state," but still the verdict is "life," though highly compromised. Families of soldiers whose fate is unknown – were they taken prisoner? could they be still alive? – are in a similar painful limbo. But in ancient Israelite and rabbinic cul-

ture, those seriously ill or wounded, or those in extreme poverty or captivity, were on the "death" end of a spectrum.

46. Heschel explains this at length in his book *The Prophets* (New York: Harper & Row, 1962).

47. Our tradition says that Rabban Gamliel in the late first century, probably around 90 C.E., oversaw the establishment of the *Amidah* prayer in basically its current form – probably using earlier precedents for communal prayer. His authority at that time extended to the academy at Yavneh and their students; but that tradition would become highly influential over the next 40 years. Still, the *Amidah* may have continued to be in flux for some time, as written prayer books were centuries in the future. By the time of the Talmud (3rd-6th centuries C.E.), the *Shemoneh esreh* was established as the weekday prayer for *shacharit, mincha,* and *ma'ariv.* It would survive without major changes - primarily slight deviations in different regions and periods - for nearly 1500 years.

48. The sketch below is adapted from that of Munk, *World of Prayer* I, pp. 124-29.

49. The Isaiah text includes "seeing with their eyes" and "hearing with their ears" as well as understanding. In the original source, this section follows on the grand temple vision of holiness of Isaiah. Other biblical passages praise knowledge and wisdom. The most likely model for blessing #4 is King Solomon's dream that he prayed for wisdom and knowledge (*chochmah u'madah*). See 2 Chronicles 1:10 and a different version in 1 Kings 3:9, where he prays for a *lev shomea*, an understanding heart (literally, "listening heart").

50. Medieval manuscripts from the Cairo Geniza show that some communities had added the word *notzrim* or Nazarenes, meaning Christians. However, we don't know whether those versions go back to as far as the early liturgy. Some scholars argue that the growth of Christianity in the late second century might have led

to adding that word; others say it was more likely local communities several centuries later who were under threat.

51. From English, we would usually expect "sprout" to refer to a plant; and it often does in Hebrew. But in the *chatimah* of blessing 15, what is sprouting or flourishing is a "horn," i.e. of an animal ("my horn You have exalted like the horn of the wild-ox," Psalms 92:11). But indeed a horn does sprout from the head as a plant from its roots. The same formulation occurs elsewhere, for example in Ezekiel 29.21, after God has declared that Nebuchadnezzar will conquer Egypt, he says, "In that day I will make a horn sprout for the house of Israel, and I will give you [the prophet] an opening of the mouth in their midst; and they shall know that I am the Lord." This is echoed in Psalms, explicitly mentioning the Davidic messiah: "There [in Zion] will I make a horn sprout for David, I have prepared a lamp for My anointed" (Psalms 132:17). An ancient metaphor has become a sign of a kingdom established by God.

52. Modern versions of the *Amidah* keep the same structure as the traditional, but in the Reform and Reconstructionist traditions, certain wordings or translations have changed. In particular, the Davidic messiah and the restoration of sacrifices are not part of the prayers in those traditions. The Reform version of the kibbutz *galiot* prayer asks for freedom for the oppressed generally, not a Jewish return to our homeland; while the Reconstructionist version retains the hope for return. We have already mentioned the issue of resurrection in the second blessing and the egalitarian language in the first. Other lesser or nuanced changes can be found in the translations while not always reflected in changes in the Hebrew text.

53. Kaplan, *Inner Space*, 153-54.

Other Gaon Books Titles
on Spirituality and Religious Practice

Gloria Abella Ballen
The Power of the Hebrew Alphabet

Levi Ben-Shmuel
Living Wisely

Tamar Frankiel
She Rises While It is Still Night: Dreaming in the Four Worlds of Kabbalah (Forthcoming)

Rabbi Min Kantrowitz
Counting the Omer: A Kabbalistic Meditation Guide

Ilan Stavans
The New World Haggadah

Rabbi Zalman Schachter-Shalomi
• *All Breathing Life Adores Your Name*
• *A Hidden Light: Stories and Teaching of Early Habad and Bratzlav Hasidim*

Susan Vorhand
The Mosaic Within: Kabbalah and Alchemy of Healing Self and Soul

Gaon Books
publishes in conjunction with the Gaon Institute, which
is a non-profit organization, designated as 501-c-3 by
the Internal Revenue Service. www.gaonnet.org